HONOR THY FATHER?
Exposing the Secret World of Incest

HONOR
THY
FATHER?

Exposing the Secret World of Incest

by Meridel Rawlings
with Jay Rawlings
as told by
JUDI

HUNTINGTON HOUSE, INC.

Shreveport • Lafayette
Louisiana

Huntington House, Inc.
P.O. Box 53788
Lafayette, Louisiana 70505

Library of Congress Catalog Card Number 86-81133
ISBN Number 0-910311-39-0

Cover by Don Ellis
Typography by Publications Technologies
Printed in the United States of America

Contents

DEDICATION:

To: Margie, Francis, Theresa, Elizabeth, Julia, Sheila, Lynne, Maxine, Wendy, Loretta, Cleo, Mary, Dusty, Skip, Carol, and Joy ... to name a few ...

AUTHOR'S NOTE:

Honor Thy Father is a true story. Names and some places have been changed to protect individual privacy.

If a thief broke into your home and stole some of your possessions, would you immediately report it to the police? Of course. But what if someone was able to break into your life and steal your feelings of self worth, cripple your ability to trust others, and trample upon your emotions — leaving you bruised with fear? What if you were a child, and that "someone" was your father or brother or grandfather or uncle?

I have written one family's story at their request, and it was my privilege to do so.

Special thanks go to Eloyse Badgett, Carol Wamsley and Jeff Sheldon for their insights and to the many who helped in a great variety of ways, including Joan Mathes, Esther McCrary, Sharon Sanders and my husband, Jay, and our three sons.

Our prayer is that no one will be the same after reading and, in a sense, reliving this family's nightmare. For those caught in a similar predicament, remember: you do not have to be a silent victim anymore!

Meridel Rawlings
Jerusalem, Israel
March, 1986

PREFACE

This book is for those who have been sexually abused and thought that they were the only ones who ever had such an experience. It is also for the mothers who feel trapped and betrayed.

We all must be taught to watch for and recognize the symptoms many times played out by victims of incest. Then it will be easier to be a detective and speak up and say, "Is something wrong? Are you in an uncomfortable situation? Do you feel badly about the way your daddy, brothers, grandfather or uncle touch you?"

Victims must be educated and encouraged to speak up and tell someone of their plight.

During the time when incest began creeping into the home of this woman "Judi," her daughters, "Trish" and "Debbie," bathed twice a day and spent an hour in the tub each time. With only one bathroom, the inconvenience would drive Judi to distraction. She just couldn't understand it.

But looking back, she can see that being sexually abused gave her girls an unclean feeling. Unconsciously they were trying to wash away their guilt and shame. If only she had known that victims do present clear symptoms which are silent cries for help, she could have picked it up before the final crisis came and perhaps could have prevented some of the remorse and agony.

Through professional counseling provided by the juvenile court, this mother of two victims learned that there is a personality trait that accompanies the molester, especially the person who abuses his own children, as a means of expressing authority. At the same time he manipulates the entire household to keep the deception covered by enforced alienation from the rest of the world. This secret is encapsulated by a terrified silence.

Unfortunately, this highly guarded practice has been prevalent from Bible times to this generation. Because our ancestors and, more recently, grandmothers, mothers and daughters have been conditioned to muteness, a web of lies and deceit has continued to be spun unhindered. Statistics today tell us that between 15 and 34 percent of all girls, and three and nine percent of all boys are victims of sexual abuse each year.[1]

Children and adults who have been driven into solitary confinement because of incest have good reason to hope. You are not alone! Call out and someone will answer. That someone could be your

---

[1]Family Violence Research Program, University of New Hampshire.

minister, friend, social worker, the police, your teacher or boyfriend. Remember, the Lord has known about it all along and is also waiting for you to call on Him and turn to Him.

"None of them that trust in Him shall be desolate," Psalm 34:22b.

Two years after our crisis came to the breaking point, Debbie and Trish attended a summer camp. Debbie, 15 years old, became very ill with a sore throat and spent her first evening alone in the dorm. Meanwhile her younger sister, 13-year-old Trish, was reprimanded for her irritable and angry response to authority. One of the youth leaders dropped in to chat with Debbie and expressed dismay over Trish's behavior. At that point in her life, Debbie was secure enough to speak openly about the damaging abuse and rape both girls had received from their father. The counselor listened intently and was deeply concerned.

The counselor's sunny disposition, and active participation in helping other youngsters of similar backgrounds, as well as seriously pursuing a professional career, had a quiet and calming effect upon Debbie.

It was a turning point in her life because she realized that life did not have to be a foregone conclusion of failure and disaster. Until then incest, as perverse and ugly as it was, sought to smother life out of her.

The counselor assured her that, if given a chance, God could work all things for good, if she was willing to talk to him. Her used and abused second-hand life could be created into an honorable and useful one. Debbie was no longer alone, or afraid.

Today she insists that the whole family was at fault to some degree for what happened to her. She requested that I look at her family and ask why and how it happened.

Then she added, "Such a terrible thing cannot happen unless the enemy of our souls steps in directly and controls the situation, which is exactly what he did."

Her personal suffering is expressed in this poem, written originally as prose some months after her father's arrest. Alterations were made by me.

> *Often I wondered,*
> *What made you do it?*
> *Hurt was skillfully,*
> *purposely inflicted ...*
> *not only upon us,*
> *but upon yourself.*
> *Evil,*
> *Degrading thoughts,*
> *written in your*
> *secret book.*
> *I read them and*
> *was Sick!*
> *Then I found out*
> *the Horror,*
> *of the sin,*
> *which you had involved*
> *me in:*
> *The hidden magazines?*
> *I was your Idol,*
> *your plaything, after*

you greedily consumed
wickedly beautiful
pictures of female bodies.
They pierced and mutilated
me with Fear,
when I first discovered them.
Your books:
The things I read
of men ...
Insane,
and what they did
secretly to their
daughters, nieces,
sisters and cousins?
Pain!
Oh Daddy
You told me
TV and movies
were nasty, wrong,
The Lies ...
I never knew
until it came clear,
with that terrible
word
Incest:
Emptiness!
To know I was nothing
more to you
my molester.
I loved you Daddy
and I wanted to help you.
You hated us!
You hated Mom,
my dear, sweet Mother
so strong and Godly

the One
you couldn't sleep with
in the same bed.
So...
you cried on my young shoulders,
Told me how
your drunk Daddy,
Hunted you with a gun,
Beat your Mom,
her whimpering
Silenced while
Blood ran!
That was before we had sex!
Your so-called
"love."
I now Despise, Detest!
You made me your Wife ...
and Ruler!
I was so young,
a child, and yet
in Control of you.
I could manipulate you,
Force you to comply
when sister and mother
failed.
Confusion and violence
filled, consumed, burned us.
Letting this happen ...
was God's fault,
you said ...
but you couldn't stop!
Satan found
and controlled your weakness.
I hated you!
I wanted to kill you.

I would beg ...
Mommy,
Please divorce him.
We have to escape.
Live a normal life.
Frustration
was driving me to
attempt Suicide.
"You'll go to hell,"
comforting words,
your Pastoral counsel.
Could it be worse
than your own
private world?
Evil and Sick?
I longed to be normal.
Torment seared my mind.
What did you think
you were doing
Father dear?
My life?
a Cesspool!
Trauma and Fear,
Frustration and Hate.
Those times
made me so sick
I was afraid
I would vomit!
Wild ... and caged.
You unleashed your
inner Torment
Lust and seed
on us all.
That twisted thing you
called "love"?

Nothing but
Fear and Hate.
Those sessions ...
Nightmares!
Honor thy father
you demanded,
I did!
I came
face to face
with the Devil!

— Meridel Rawlings

THE END

"... Oh say, can you see,
by the dawn's early light,
What so proudly we hailed
at the twilight's last gleaming,
Whose broad stripes and bright
stars, thru the perilous fight ..."

Brass trumpets accompanied the words of the
American national anthem like a broken record in
my mother-in-law's mind. It was still and hot and
2 a.m., July 5th. A blanket of oppressive heat drove
sleep away. Stella reached out and snapped on the
bedside lamp.

Her blistered feet served as an unpleas-
ant reminder that the 4th of July celebration spent
with our family had been decidedly exhausting. She
was bone-weary from her gallant effort to attend all

four parades in which our girls — her grand-daughters Debbie and Trish — had played flute and clarinet.

Through her tired mind marched scores of Boy and Girl Scouts, elaborately decorated floats, cowboys, Indians, streamers, balloons and clowns. Her nerves had been frayed by the time we reached the picnic grounds for a hamburger barbecue served up by my husband, Larry, her eldest son.

"At home on the East Coast it's 3 a.m. now," Stella mused to herself, fluffing up her pillow. "I've been in Nebraska just a month and still haven't adjusted to the time difference."

Slowly she swung her tired legs over the side of the bed and her swollen feet found their way into worn slippers. Pulling on her bathrobe, she decided to get a drink and inched carefully along the hall-way in the darkness towards the kitchen.

"A glass of water and some sleeping pills will help," she reasoned and turned on the tap.

Then she heard a sound — thud, thud.

"That's strange," she mused. "Did I hear something? Are they still shooting off fireworks at this hour?"

She lifted a slat in the venetian blind and peered out at the dark street in front of the house. The park across the way was empty, silent. Then she heard it again — thud, thud, thud. The muffled sound was coming from somewhere in the house.

"Maybe someone has broken in," she thought.

Her pulse quickening, she stepped deliberately from the kitchen, back into the hall. She stopped, got her direction and listened. There was light leaking around the closed basement door.

It wasn't just hatred, it was a sickening disgust. If he had not been between me and the shotgun in the closet, I know that I would have killed him.

Yet in a calm, deliberate voice, I said, "Larry, the authority that you have had over me and the children is finished. There is no way in this world that you will ever have any authority over us again. I've lived by what you've said, and I've done what you asked and what you insisted to the point of being ridiculous."

My voice quivered as I continued. "You have devastated my child. How could you even imagine that I would ever trust you again? From now on you'll do what I tell you to do and we'll do what I think is best and I don't care what your opinion is. I'm sick of being told what to do and how to live and when to shut up. I just can't believe that you would do this to my child."

"Judi, everything is fine, I don't know what you are so upset about," he said meekly.

I was so angry I could barely speak.

Then his mother, Stella, called him and he turned silently away and went downstairs.

I sank onto the bed. I began to understand. Fragments that had puzzled me for years began to form a very pathetic mosaic before my eyes.

Incest!

Debbie lay sobbing, huddled beside me, "Mother, didn't you know?"

"No dear."

My voice was distant, unemotional. I was hearing my old, repeated advice playing back. "You girls ought to honor your father. Be proud of him. You've got a good daddy, he's a preacher, and he

"Maybe it's coming from the basement," she thought as she tiptoed forward.

Quietly turning the doorknob to investigate, she opened the door.

A lone, dim light bulb bathed the steep wooden stairs in a weak yellow aura.

The eerie noise was louder.

Stella's arthritic fingers clung to the wooden rail. Bracing herself, she descended a few steps. Cautiously, she peered into one darkened corner and then the other. She found it difficult to focus without her glasses. The basement was unfinished and used for storage, a pantry, Larry's study and homemade gym. She peered back and forth.

Then, she saw.

Her heart lunged so hard she thought surely it would stop. Her stomach knotted and sent a flow of bile upwards into her mouth. It was bitter, sour.

Over against the wall, 15 feet from the bottom of the stairs, lay her beloved 36-year-old son, Larry, having sex with her 15-year-old granddaughter, Debbie.

Horrified, Stella understood the noise.

But she refused to believe what she saw.

"No!" her reeling mind tried to reason. "No, no, it's a nightmare. I must wake up!"

In disbelief, she trembled on the stairs — yet dared not turn away for fear that she would be heard. Perspiration welled on her forehead and the back of her neck, but her palms were cold, dead.

She was petrified — disbelieving, unable to even think.

The scene could not be real. As she turned to go back upstairs, she staggered — bumping a glass jar on the step.

As if in slow motion, it flipped end over end toward the basement's concrete floor. Stella stared, mesmerized. Then it hit the floor and shattered.

The crash brought her son to an embarrassed halt.

Stella gasped. Her eyes met her son's.

"Oh, Mother —" Larry tried to sound nonchalant as he swung over onto the side of the bed. Debbie leapt up, threw on her nightie and flew barefooted up the steps, past her grandmother.

She ran down the front hall of the townhouse, until, panting and terrified, she collapsed at the side of my king-size bed, and shook me as I slept.

"Wake up, Momma. You have to wake up. Grandma Stella just found Daddy having sex with me."

Slowly opening my eyes, "She what?" I asked groggily.

"You heard me, Momma," Debbie pleaded. "You know what I mean. She found Daddy having sex with me."

"Grandma Stella? She found Daddy ... *what?*"

"Mother —" Debbie erupted into tears.

I struggled up, awkwardly holding her in my arms.

"Debbie?" I whispered as calmly as possible.

But an explosion was going off inside my head. My world was reeling.

"I don't know what all of this is about Debbie," I whispered. Spontaneously I put my hands on her head and prayed, "Oh God —" Then I faltered. "I can't even think," I protested to the Lord.

I clutched my trembling, weeping daughter. "Daddy said you knew," Debbie repeated, tears streaming down her face. "Daddy said —"

"Debbie," I interrupted. "I didn't know a thing. Stay here."

Downstairs, Stella was in the living room. La was standing next to her, speaking very quietly.

"Larry," I exclaimed, my voice even, "I want talk to you in the bedroom immediately."

Turning, I went back upstairs. On our be Debbie was shivering uncontrollably. Meekly, Lar stared at her.

"Larry," I challenged, "Debbie just told me th Stella found you having sex with her. Is that true'

Shuffling his feet, avoiding my eyes, Lar blurted, "Judi, as long as we love each other and a like everything is OK, it's going to be fine."

"No it will not!" My voice cracked wi emotion. "It's not fine now and it's not going to fine no matter what you say. I didn't believe yo could do this to our child."

"Judi, I didn't do anything."

"Larry!" I shouted, "Debbie just said ..."

"Mother, he did!" Debbie cried out from tl bed. "Daddy, tell Momma what you did. He w having sex with me."

"Larry, did you?"

"Judi."

"Is that all you can do, look at me and sa 'Judi'?"

"As long as we act like everything is all righ everything will be fine," he repeated.

My instincts as a woman and mother instantl told me that this whole mess was out of my hand My husband was not reasoning and had not bee reasonable for 17 years. He could not understan why I was upset.

Any vestige of love for him had just died.

loves you and comes home every night. He doesn't smoke, drink or run around with women."

A wave of nausea ripped through me. "Why should he run around with women?" I whispered to myself. "He was jumping into bed with my child."

"Daddy always told me that you knew," Debbie repeated.

"Debbie, oh, Debbie," I said, holding her close. "Do you think for a moment I would let him touch you like that if I had known? Of course I didn't know. He was lying to you."

Debbie's sobs shook the bed. Then she breathed deeply and quieted. "Oh, Mother, I'm sorry, I'm so sorry." Her cry was intense and wounded.

"I'm sorry too, dear, and I'm going to make sure that this gets all straightened out," I promised. "You don't have to suffer for this any longer. Don't worry, he'll never touch you again."

Debbie began to cry so hard that she almost retched. Her eyes were swollen. Her mouth and nose were red.

"Mother," she wept. "I'm *sorry.*"

"Debbie, it's not your fault! Look at me." I took her trembling chin in my hand and held it firmly. I stared deeply into eyes that betrayed deep wounds. "Listen to me very carefully. I love you. You can stop crying, because he is never going to touch you again. Can you believe me?"

Debbie barely nodded her head. "I'm going to make sure that you get to a doctor and things are going to be taken care of."

Debbie gently whispered, "Thanks, Mom," and turned over and tried to sleep.

Larry was still talking to his mother.

I didn't feel comfortable interrupting them, so I waited.

I continued to piece together what had been going on — and what had just taken place. For months, I'd been trying to understand gnawing inconsistencies, but nothing had fit.

Now they did.

Back in March I had prayed desperately, "O Lord, show me what's wrong." It had been so obvious that things were not right between Larry and me. "Show me what to do," I had prayed. "Let me know, so that I can straighten it out. I'm sick of living such a frustrated life and I know that it's not your will ... show me."

I knew that God had always been faithful to me and had answered my prayers. I searched my soul and asked God to show me what to do. I had no idea how to handle this terrible situation. I was hurt so badly I couldn't think.

My mind rejected it — to think my husband was that low or sick to have molested, abused and used my precious daughter.

We all knew that he and Debbie never got along. Their natures seemed to be so different. She was so strong willed. I remember her sitting in his lap and loving him. Then the next instant she would jump up, screaming obscenities at him.

Now I understood why he had had the vasectomy and why he had insisted on showing the girls his stitches. I thought it pretty sick at the time. Then I remembered Debbie's vaginal infection. Then it hit me — Trish, my youngest daughter, had suffered from the infection and so had I.

Little Trish?

My tired mind raced — Trish? No!

Then, I saw the faces of foster children who had come through our home: Frances, Mary Lou, Margie, Theresa.

All previously hurt and abused.

Now, Debbie was acting just like them.

Deep hurt too deep to express racked my spirit, soul and body. I curled up in a grip of pure agony.

I was reduced to nothing.

The awful, terrible truth was there for me to acknowledge. The very thing that made me so furious in the lives of others had invaded my own home.

Around 4:30 a.m., Larry stood in the bedroom door. Dawn was breaking and the birds had begun to twitter.

I stared at him, red-eyed.

"Larry, the children are going to a doctor tomorrow," I whispered, not wanting to disturb Debbie beside me.

"Oh, no," he answered. "Why would you want to do that? Debbie is fine. There's nothing wrong with her."

"She is going to the doctor." I threw the words at him.

"No, I don't want her to go."

"I don't care what you want, it doesn't matter to me." I declared. "She needs help."

"Oh, there's nothing wrong with our little Debbie."

"Are you crazy?" I spat.

"Judi, how can you say that? Debbie is a fine child."

"She was," I rasped between clinched teeth.

"But, Judi." Larry was beginning to show concern, "as long as we love each other and act like everything is going to be OK, it's going to be fine. Why, things are going good now."

I gazed at him in disgust. Deep inside, I knew the whole situation was out of my hands. The girls had to have medical help and professional counseling. As a result, legal authorities would be contacted.

And I had no desire to protect Larry at the continued risk of my girls. I also knew that unless Larry realized the scope of his problem, there really was not much that could be done for him, either.

I closed my eyes.

"Larry," I said, exhausted, "I don't know whether you have worn me out, or have used up all my love, or whether you just have hurt me so badly I cannot recover. I don't know, because I am numb from the inside out. I do know this, you will never, never touch me again, and I will not allow you ever to be near my child again. Do you hear me, Larry?"

"Judi, why do you always exaggerate everything? Nothing is wrong, for goodness sake." He seemed to have no comprehension of what he had done.

He knew I was angry, but actually didn't seem to understand why. There seemed to be absolutely no recognition that what he had done was dreadfully wrong.

"Larry." My blue eyes leveled on him. He didn't move. "If you ever so much as touch Debbie again, you will be dead."

"Why, Judi, I'll do anything you want. Just don't be so upset about it." He walked away and went downstairs.

In a daze, I got off of the bed and went down to the kitchen to fix some coffee. Stella was still up, too. I didn't say anything to her.

I didn't know what to say.

After drinking a cup of coffee, I dressed for work. I had to go to work. I was our family's bread-winner. Larry could have never held a steady job — nor a pastorate, although he was an ordained minister.

I pondered my next move. How could I leave the girls in the house with him? As impossible as it seems now, I didn't believe I had any choice that morning. I didn't know what else to do.

I awakened Debbie and whispered, "Just take it easy. I'll be home right after work and will take care of everything."

"Mother," she asked groggily, "tomorrow I have band practice early. Can I go?"

The request seemed incredible.

Band practice? Tomorrow?

"Sure, why not?" I heard myself saying.

"Daddy said I couldn't go because he was punishing me."

I stared at her silently. Then, as calmly as possible, "Debbie, I'm your mother," I said. "Your dad doesn't have any authority over you anymore. I'll drive you there myself."

"But it's 7 o'clock in the morning, Mom."

"Suits me. You be good and you practice today. I'll be home right after work."

In the kitchen, I found that Larry was up, dressed and ready for work — he was currently employed as a clerk at a toy store.

He seemed completely untroubled by the early morning's events.

As he drove me to the medical center where I worked, I was still struggling to sort everything out.

"Larry, do you realize what you have done?"

"Well, maybe we could go to the zoo this weekend," he answered inanely. "Maybe we could take the kids to Nebraska City."

"Larry," I shouted, "you don't understand!"

"Judi." He reached over and laid his huge, heavy hand on my knee. "You don't have any reason to be upset. Everything is going to be fine."

Jerking away from him, I replied, "Larry, you don't understand what is going on."

"Judi, I think we could have a good time this weekend."

He pulled over in front of the medical center. I got out, slammed the door and walked toward the office, still in shock. The ground beneath me seemed to be moving. My knees were shaky.

I struggled for strength to pull my mind into my work as a receptionist, greeting the public and answering the telephone. Silently I prayed and fought back the tears.

The inner sickness I felt still had not lifted at noon when the telephone rang.

"Good afternoon, Dr. Martin's office."

"Judi, how you doing?" Larry asked.

"Larry, did you really have intercourse with her?" I whispered.

"I don't see why you are so upset about it."

"Larry, answer me!"

"Oh, Judi, Debbie's fine."

Nauseous, I slammed the phone down. Every time I thought of the situation, I felt sicker.

I tried to keep busy all afternoon but nothing could block out the pain. Every time I would relax even for a second, the gruesome events kept coming back into my mind.

By closing time, I was on the verge of rage, convinced that I could choke him with my bare hands.

When Larry drove up in front of the medical center to pick me up, he leaned over and opened the door. Smiling, "Did you have a good day?" he asked.

"Larry, I don't believe you did that."

"Come on, what's the matter, Judi? Why do you keep going on? Everything is going to be fine."

"Larry, you must apologize to Debbie for what you've done."

"Oh, sure, I'd be glad to do that."

We drove home in silence.

His study was in the basement next to where her temporary bed had been. Suddenly, I blurted that I wanted him to tell her he was sorry. "I expect you to make it an honest apology," I spat at him. "She desperately needs to know that what you did to her was *wrong*. Do you understand me, Larry? Wrong!"

"Sure, Judi," he agreed, as we pulled into the driveway. "Can I take the girls swimming this evening?"

"Over my dead body."

"Well, Judi, maybe you could come swimming, too."

"I don't want you near my children!"

I knew I needed some time to think — to figure out what to do.

As I entered the house, Stella put her hand under my elbow and drew me aside. "Dear, I need to speak with you," she whispered.

"OK," I agreed. In the next breath I commanded, "Larry, talk to Debbie now."

They went downstairs to his study. Letting Stella wait, I stood quietly at the top of the stairs and listened.

"Debbie, I'm concerned that you aren't practicing your flute enough," Larry told her.

"I'm going to 7 o'clock practice tomorrow, Daddy, and it's going well."

"When is your next basketball practice?"

"They are over for the summer."

"Well, I'm proud of you and you have lots of potential and I expect you to live up to all that we have taught you."

"I'll do my best, Daddy."

"When do you deliver papers?"

"At 5 p.m."

"Well, it's after five. You and Trish better get a move on."

Stunned, I realized he wasn't sorry. I knew that he *couldn't* care or understand. It burned me as I painfully saw that he never would be sorry. He was not capable of understanding the seriousness of what he had done. Yet the damage had been done — and it was such *extensive damage*.

I remembered the faces of Frances and Margie, two little foster children that we had taken in. They were emotional cripples and retarded because of sexual abuse by their mother's boyfriends. I remembered how upset we all were because the psychiatrist and psychologist said that their emotional damage was so severe that they would never be mentally or emotionally normal again.

Sadness pervaded my soul. Grief worked its way in and with it came depression.

When Larry and Debbie came upstairs, I turned to Larry and said, "You can take the girls swimming for one hour and if you aren't back I'll come and personally get you."

I realized I was threatening him. But I meant every word of it. "You girls can go swimming with your dad for one hour, but he is not to lay a finger on you, do you hear?"

"Momma," Debbie whined, "we understand, but I have to tell you, I don't like staying here with Grandma Stella. She keeps looking at me like I'm dirt. Every time she saw me today, she made me feel like I was the scum of the earth and I can't stand her treating me ugly. She says it's all my fault. I'm not going to stay with her."

"Go on, girls, I'll discuss it with you later. Go and deliver your papers and go swimming."

When the house was quiet, Stella and I sat down over a cup of coffee. I wanted to have a heart-to-heart discussion with her.

She told me how that she had found Larry with Debbie. She shook her head as she shared her horror and disgust. "Judi, I'm so sick over this, I don't know what to do."

"I don't know what to do, either," I answered as I plucked withered and dead leaves from my African violet.

"What can you do but divorce him?" Thin veins on her temples stood out. Her voice was sad.

"Stella, I don't want to get into that now. I have to take care of the children for the moment."

She took a sip of coffee. "You better check Trish. I think he has bothered them both."

Suddenly, I knew I needed help. Professional help. Medical help. Legal help.

Larry and the girls came back and we had supper. I tried to keep calm. Stella volunteered to handle the dishes. Trish, Debbie and I went into the bedroom. I closed the door.

"Trish, Daddy will never touch Debbie again. He no longer has any power over us. Did Daddy ever bother you?"

Trish lowered her eyes and slowly nodded her blond curls. She had just reached puberty at age 13.

"Uh huh," she muttered affirmatively.

I grew silently livid.

"Trish, tell me, did he really touch you?"

"Uh huh, sure Mom." Then, suddenly she flared defensively. "What's the big deal?"

"Trish, daddies aren't supposed to do that!"

"But he said that you knew all about it and that's what we were for."

The horror of the lie shook me.

"Trish?" My voice broke. Tears ran unashamedly down my face. "Trish, that is a lie. Your daddy lied, do you understand that?"

She stared into my eyes, unembarrassed.

I trembled, knowing that my husband had turned this little girl into a woman.

"Girls, we'll go down to the basement now and get Debbie's bed, change the sheets, and put it in here beside your bed, Trish. Keep your door closed. Do not leave your room and if your father comes to the door, call out and I'll come."

Righteous indignation filled me with strength. I walked deliberately into the living room and announced, "Larry, I need to be alone."

He quietly took a book and went upstairs.

I sat down in the rocking chair that had been his favorite place to sit with the girls on his lap.

"If only I had known. If only ...." The words echoed in my mind. I took the Yellow Pages and began to thumb through them. I didn't know what to do, who to turn to, or where to go.

I only knew that I had to do something — and I had to do it fast.

The events had shattered my world, and I didn't know how to dig out from under the rubble.

In the front of the phone book, I ran my finger down hot line numbers. Then I noticed there was a number to call for child abuse.

It was a toll-free number. I prayed for guidance, picked up the receiver and dialed.

"Hello, may I help you?" a voice asked.

"Yes." I swallowed, trying to be as quiet as possible, not wanting Larry to know what I was doing. "I've just found out that my girls are being abused and I don't know what to do."

"Well, first let me suggest that you call your minister and talk to him."

"Thank you." I hung up.

We'd been going to a nearby church. Larry was a licensed minister in that denomination, so I didn't feel that I could face the pastor to tell him the ugly things I had to say.

Then I remembered another minister. Ever since Stella had been with us, we had attended his small church in a village near our home. He seemed to be a reasonable man. I knew he'd had years of seminary training and would be educated.

I glanced at my watch. It was already 11 p.m. Again I prayed as I dialed.

It rang twice.

"Good evening," a kindly voice said.

"Hello," I said, identifying myself. "I desperately need to speak with you. We attended your services recently, and I just felt I could talk to you." I was sure he sensed my urgency. "I need to speak with you early tomorrow, but I must be at work by 8:30."

"Fine, I'll meet you in my office tomorrow at 7 a.m. Do you know where it is?"

"Yes, sir, it's just off of the sanctuary as you enter the church."

"That's right. See you then."

"Thank you," I said.

I hung up the receiver and cried.

I couldn't imagine what to do next. The pain consumed me.

As I dragged myself upstairs, my body seemed an unbearable weight. I got into my nightie and laid down beside the man who for 17 years had been my husband.

Tentatively, he turned toward me.

"Judi."

"Shut up," I ordered. "Turn back over, I don't want to ever look at your face again."

"What's wrong now?" He sounded like a six-year-old. "Why are you so mad?"

I was so hurt I couldn't even begin to answer. I just laid there and cried — and cried. It was to be another sleepless night.

I was tortured.

I hurt so badly to think that my children had been damaged.

The night melted away as I rehashed one anguished memory after another.

I was on the rack.

This was what the Inquisition must have been like.

No words can describe my pain and sorrow.

All I could see was endless destruction.

The devil had come in like a roaring lion and had trampled over the two most precious beings in my life. I no longer fought the awful realization that the man laying beside me was too sick for me to cope with.

Throughout 17 years of marriage, I had convinced myself, "If I try harder, maybe he'll be happy."

Now, I was reduced to emptiness.

Larry's heavy, even breathing let me know that he was sound asleep, convinced that everything was fine.

2

THIS IS MY LIFE

I lied to my husband. Debbie and I left the house just before 7 a.m. I explained that I was taking her to band practice and would watch her practice. But I didn't tell the whole truth.

After dropping her off, I drove over to the church and made my way to the pastor's office. Apprehensively I knocked at the door of his study, which was slightly open.

"Please come in," he said, calling my name.

His voice filled me with reassurance and gratitude.

He was not what one would call attractive.

Pock marks scarred his face, but his clear, gentle eyes and an open smile reassured me that he was a man of God in his own way. A quiet strength enveloped him, giving him the dignity of a wise man.

As I sat back in a comfortable armchair across from his desk, I began to weep. I couldn't speak.

Slowly, I whispered, "My daughter awakened me in the middle of the night and said, 'Grandma found Daddy having sex with me.' "

Emotion choked me and I sat mute, staring helplessly at the pastor.

"First of all, let's pray." The pastor leaned forward. I nodded in agreement, too overcome to do anything except blow my nose and wipe my eyes.

"Dear Heavenly Father, your word says that you care especially for the widow and the fatherless. Please send strong help to this family in their time of deep distress. Amen! Tell me about your family."

I tried to compose myself, and hesitatingly began to speak. "Well, sir, originally, we are from the East Coast. I was raised in a minister's home. My family loved one another, but were never very good at openly showing affection. From an early age I was taught to care for my father and brothers and my relationship revolved around what I could do to help them."

Then I floundered, blushing, not being accustomed to this kind of direct personal attention.

"It's OK, now tell me about your husband," he quietly requested.

"Well, I met him in the study hall at high school. He was six feet, five inches tall, good looking, intelligent, and I remember him as very intense. We shared the same study period and never did homework, just talked. He told me that he was writing a book entitled *Do You Believe the Bible Is True?* I was impressed. Willingly, I typed his manuscript and it was rather monotonous. At times I felt uneasy with him, and found him headstrong, disorganized and even disoriented. He would say things that worried me like, "I sleep with a knife under my pillow." One day he shocked me by saying, "Judi, do you masturbate?" I tried not to show my naiveté and answered "No!"

" 'Well,' he said, 'I do and sometimes I worry because I think it will drive me insane.' I couldn't think of anything to answer. I should have known right then that he was not the man for me. He had two younger brothers and there was no friendship between them. Each lived in his own world. They kept everything separate and didn't know how to share. At Christmastime their father, who was an alcoholic, tried to give bigger and better presents than the year before. He had grown up in poverty and insisted that they have every material benefit. He literally killed himself with alcohol and overwork but provided a fine home in the best part of town.

"As a child, Larry saw his mother, in fits of rage, scratch her face until it bled. She told me that Larry was sickly at birth because of a blood factor. He has a very poor immunity system, and was a weak baby. As a result of his repeated sickness, he was overly indulged."

My mouth felt like it was full of cotton, but I continued. "When Larry was 18 he decided he wanted to serve God. He said that his life had changed and we began to date more frequently.

"Once during high school he was scheduled to participate in the state track meet. The day arrived and he was too sick to think of running but prayed for help, found enough strength to go on and won the mile run, becoming the state high school champion. I must say I was impressed and enjoyed all of the attention that comes with being the best girl of a track star.

"That summer after graduation we both went to youth camp together and Larry insisted that we get married. However, I resisted because I was preparing for college. He threatened to commit suicide if we didn't marry. I became convinced, but carried a real load of guilt. That was when I began to slip under the false responsibility for his depression. I believed that he would change and I also decided that I hadn't given our relationship a fair chance."

Again, tears welled up in my eyes as I realized what a fool I'd been.

"Our parents were not in favor of the wedding. However, Larry's dad paid for everything. We didn't need to work. Larry attended college that fall, and I began a dental assistant's program. He had a track scholarship but couldn't handle the stress of workouts and long study hours. So, he quit college after the first semester. At that time I remember his mother visited us and ripped him up one side and down the other for quitting school. I think she effectively planted a tiny seed of failure in him, because he could never come up to her expectations, which has plagued him to this day.

"Then he just started copping out and it has never stopped.

"We moved to Tucson, Arizona, where Larry took a job selling encyclopedias for two weeks. But he couldn't stand the rejection associated with salesmanship and quit. Then he applied to join the Army but changed his mind before his papers were processed.

"I became increasingly upset about his inability to follow through on anything. He called his father who sent money to help us.

"We moved back to New Jersey and into his parents' basement for a couple of months. During that time, one day I found his mother unconscious from a drug overdose and called an ambulance. She was furious with me for foiling her plans to kill herself and involving the police. I also learned that Larry once had psychiatric care at age 13 for suicidal tendencies."

The more I talked the easier it became and he was a good listener.

"Larry received a full, four-year track scholarship to a university. Larry's dad bought us a new car and things seemed really bright.

"A year after we were married I got pregnant and Larry began to battle bouts of dark depression. It worried me and I'd wonder why he couldn't bounce back and keep his mind straight.

"Debbie, our first daughter, arrived and she was the first grandchild on both sides of the family. Everyone was so proud. She was the first child born to any students attending the university, which was a relatively new school. She was really special. Both Larry's mother and grandmother came to stay with us. That put more work on me for I waited on them as well as Larry and the baby. When the baby was only six weeks old, we were in such a bind financially I had to find a babysitter and return to work. It was very hard for Larry to have me go back and resume financial responsibilities.

"One wintery afternoon in March, I came home from work to find him alone with the baby. He had gone berserk, smashing dishes, lamps and pictures.

He broke some things that I really loved. The baby was screaming with terror and I went to comfort her. He insisted that his work load was too heavy and wanted to quit. I got angry and said, 'Not again!' In blind rage he struck me and almost broke my arm. I grabbed the baby and fled out to the car. Inwardly I thought 'If only I could drive, we would escape to New Jersey.' The sad fact is I stayed in the car until about eleven that night. That was the first time I really knew a disturbed person. I also knew that if I left him he'd be unable to cope and I made a deliberate decision to stick it out.

"The following years were filled with Larry's part-time jobs and living in our parents' basements or apartments. Larry worked for a box company, as a mail clerk wherever he could find work. Those were days of gloom. By that time I was expecting our second child.

"For years I heard a small voice inside that would command me, 'Work harder' and I thought that if I was more patient we could work it out. Larry was a clerk at Woolco and quit when Trish, our second daughter, was one month old. Our parents gave us money. He worked one year at a 7-Eleven store and then became the manager, putting in 70 to 80 hours a week. The stress was heavy, and we were making just enough to pay bills. I stayed home with the little girls and sold Tupperware. He took a part-time job as a security guard and became furious with me when I sang in the church choir and worked in a Girl Scout troop. I believe he was jealous for my affections. When he was home he needed and demanded my absolute attention.

"He loved to play with the children and would play ball and run through the house, but he couldn't stand the mess they made. When they were two and four years old he wrote up a list of rules and read them to the girls every day. We thought it was kind of cute. 'Play in your room, put your toys away, etc.'

"He told me frequently that I made him unhappy because I was fat. He knew how to beat me down with his mouth in a hundred different ways. I could never win. There was no way I could get my way out of any of the arguments and recognized that I had a mess on my hands. Later he began to accuse me of every sin in the world.

"Nine years ago he decided he wanted to be a minister. We'd sold all that we had and made ourselves available for the Lord to use us. He became the assistant pastor in a tiny country church and quit after three months, packed us into the car and went home to his parents.

"However, all was not lost. He applied for ministry in another denomination. He found out that he could pastor during the year and attend seminary courses at a university in the summer until he was fully ordained. We were encouraged. The girls and I wanted him to be happy, and he really wanted to be a preacher. I was determined to be supportive. I knew how frustrating and disgusting a job it would be to be a pastor's wife. My mother had been one most of her life. I also knew that it was not my job, but God's.

By now I was calmed down. The gentle pastor smiled at me as I continued the story.

"Larry's mother was very pleased at the prospect of being the mother of a preacher. She believed that he finally would make something of himself. She let us know that he had drained her all of his life. Now it was time for him to do his part. I found her a malicious busybody and after nine years of marriage I still felt that way.

"That fall Larry's dad died and his mother again attempted suicide, twice. Larry had stopped talking suicide but now everything was my fault. He could take no responsibility and everything had to be perfect. 'If I just worked harder', I thought. Looking back now I see that I met his physical needs but never began to touch the deep spiritual void in his life. I pitied him when I should have given a push along with my prayer.

"When the girls were very young, Larry insisted on reading to them and it began a habit that carried on right up into their teens. Both girls became fluent readers at an early age and as they grew, instead of Daddy reading to them they read to him. Their book shelves were lined with *Encyclopedia Brown*, the *Beverly Cleary* books such as *Ramona the Pest* and *Henry Huggins*. C. S. Lewis's *The Lion, The Witch and The Wardrobe* was a favorite as was the *Little House On the Prairie* series.

"I realized that the girls were conditioned from infancy to go to Daddy for everything. It created an imbalance that slowly grew over the years leaving me as the maid and cook rather than mother. I unconsciously allowed it.

"We waited on him hand and foot. After bathing he would leave his soaking wet towel on the bed and if the bed got wet, he would blame me. At night before going to bed, he slowly would take off one sock and lay back and toss it across the room. Then he would slowly peel off the second one and do likewise.

"He was always angry over who kept the checkbook or who paid the bills. I would give him the bills and the checks but he couldn't make up his mind when to pay what. We argued every month because I'd wait till the last minute and write out the checks for electricity and rent and go and pay them. I was usurping his God-given authority, he said.

"Our girls were also wearing down under the stress. Debbie was hyperactive and overly sensitive. Trish was the opposite, absolutely complacent, taking up to three naps a day. I took them to the doctor for a complete medical exam and they each had 20 different allergies.

"I'll never forget the day Larry got his minister's license. Now things would change for the better, I was convinced. He was given the charge of two rural churches. Happily we unloaded all of our earthly belongings from our old Ford into a sweet little white house that sat next to a quaint stone church on a circular drive. There was an ancient cemetery on the far side. We had a beautiful view of rolling hills from the front bay window and the house was very adequate with two bedrooms, study, built-in basement and big, fenced-in back yard.

"The church folks were friendly and brought us food, making us feel welcome. After just a few weeks there we became aware of strain that existed between the two churches. However, we all pitched into our new life with great enthusiasm, and even planted a garden. I learned to can vegetables. We got a dog and the kids made lots of friends with the neighbors. There was a horse next door that they could ride, and life, for the first time since we were married, seemed grand.

"Larry continued to attend the university to work toward his ordination papers and also seemed released and at peace. There was just one thing wrong in the house. Mildew covered the basement walls. Full of enthusiasm, I washed it all out with a good disinfectant and made a playroom for the girls. Immediately I contracted hives and my eyes swelled up. It was so bad I should have been hospitalized. But I refused as I knew Larry couldn't manage without me. I realized that stress complicated it all but I didn't know how to work out a reasonable solution because if I didn't hold things together they would come unglued.

"Larry developed a serious chest cold that spring. His mother came and stayed four months which was a strain on me. By summertime Larry still was too sick to sit up. We took him to the hospital. They found fungus in his lungs which was caused by the mildew in the basement. The girls and I drove 250 miles one way to see him in the hospital. It was difficult because now I was responsible for the ministry.

"When he was released from the hospital he had to spend the summer at his mother's to recuperate. He was no longer physically able to return to the university to work on the seminary courses.

"I did the visitation, organized various ministries and cooked at the summer school. It was a long summer. Larry returned in the fall, physically weakened. He preached and visited three times a week. But nothing I could do pleased him. He told me I wasn't as good as his mother. She moved in with us again. His grandmother even came to stay with us and caring for them all left me exhausted. The children and I were going in circles. Our lives revolved around keeping them all happy.

"I had no point of reference for 'normalcy'. Exhaustion and dissatisfaction became a way of life. Sometimes the sun did shine down when we were able to touch needy lives and see people transformed through a knowledge of who Jesus is and what He had done for them. We do have some very precious memories woven among the pain and darkness.

"Larry wearied of pastoring. He said he was tired of answering to the authority of a local church. He was often depressed and wanted to quit. Consequently we moved out of the parsonage. He became a traveling evangelist while I held the family together by working full time as a general practitioner's nurse. We were given the use of a hunter's cottage up in the woods. It had no running water, or bathroom and I used to heat the water for dishes and baths in a 50-cup coffee urn. Larry preached 10 times in 18 months and the rest of the time enjoyed playing, hiking and swimming with the girls.

"I began to realize that I was wearing out fast. My body and mind were exhausted and strangely numb. That winter we took in the first of many foster children. I didn't want to take them in but Larry insisted.

"Our first was a 16-year-old-boy whose father was in jail for murder. The father was considered to be the terror of the county. Friends said we were risking our lives by taking in the boy. It meant more responsibility for me and I was already overworked. It seemed our entire lives were backward.

"One day Larry walked in and announced that we were moving to a small town to take a pastorate. I could not help Larry in the ministry because he could not stand for me to make any suggestions, no matter how small. It was his work and he didn't want me to interfere. I had a full-time job caring for our two girls and within a short time, seven foster children.

"Our family problems came to a head when I signed a contract to be the cook at a camp for underprivileged children. Larry and the church board gave me permission. I took the children and we looked forward to a good time at the lake away from the restriction of city life.

"During that summer Larry became vicious and demanded that I come home. I refused. It was the first time I ever had withstood him with a direct 'No.' He insisted that the girls go home with him for a week or two and then come to camp for a week and return home the following week. He accused me of having an affair with one of the teenage boys at the campground. It was another long summer.

"Upon returning to the parsonage in time to put all of the kids into school, Larry announced that he had quit! I was shocked, as the church provided our home and paid the utilities. It was literally our livelihood. We had no idea what to do or where to go, then my sister Theresa called and said, 'Come to Nebraska.' We did.

"Overnight we packed up and moved halfway across the country. We had no specific reason to go to Nebraska, other than my sister had already rented a townhouse for us. It was a chance to leave the past behind. Larry drove a U-Haul truck which towed one of our cars and I drove the other. I was happy that I didn't have to listen to him the whole trip and only had to cope with him at meal times. I was free from his criticism, if only for a short time.

"It was a blessing to have the house ready for us, thanks to my sister. She lived in the same building complex. We both went job hunting that first week. I found work as a dental assistant and Larry found a job a month later during the Christmas rush in a toy store. The girls were busy at school. We began to attend a large church. It was hard not being the minister's wife. Yet I enjoyed the release from responsibility. I also enjoyed my new work which allowed me to meet the public and be a part of the outside world.

"The girls wanted to join the school band, so I called a pawn shop and got a $30 flute. I borrowed the money for the flute from my brother-in-law. I paid him back at $5 a month. Then we bought a clarinet for Trish, the same way, and the instruments turned out to be a wonderful diversion for the girls.

"Larry was driving us all crazy. He was angry 24 hours a day. His anger boiled, consuming him like a volcano. It seeped through the crust in vicious verbal abuse, or, at other times, it exploded violently destroying everything in its wake. We never were able to learn what would trigger it. He couldn't do anything for himself. He could not be left alone. He needed to be cared for. Suddenly he became interested in body-building. Mr. Universe became his idol. All of his extra money went into weights and muscle-building magazines.

"One afternoon, Debbie came crying to me, 'Momma, what are we going to do with Daddy, he's driving me crazy, nothing I do pleases him, and he's never happy.'

"I knew it better than she. I also knew that you don't divorce a preacher. I had been his mother for so long. I didn't know anything else to do. But our lives were becoming more and more tense. My girls were growing up, but Larry wasn't.

"One night at the supper table, Trish gave a play on words and I joked with her. We both giggled gleefully. Larry snapped, 'Will you shut up, you sound like a child!'

" 'I was just playing with the kids!' I said.

" 'It's not your job to play with the kids, you're their mother, and this is no place to play so just shut up!'

"I sat in a hurt silence alone while he got up from the table and called to the girls to go and play a game in the living room. We were growing apart. Anytime the girls would try to involve me he would ridicule the idea. It got so that I would do anything to escape. So I'd go to the library and read.

"In time Larry was promoted to manager of the toy store. He was tired from the long hours of struggling, but doing well, and we were all proud of him. I thought maybe there was a change. Things were looking better. The girls began their fall semester of school and we had a little money to buy them the things they needed. In mid-September Larry walked in and announced, 'I quit my job today.' "

When I briefly hesitated, he encouraged me to continue.

"I was heartbroken. We were turning in a vicious circle. Larry didn't realize that when he quit he had no right to unemployment insurance, or any other kind of help. My job wasn't making that much! The kids and I were dizzy from going round and round. We couldn't make Larry happy. Nothing worked, nothing! Now when the girls came home from school he was home every day. When I walked in from work, Debbie was in tears or Trish was furious because they'd been fighting each other. They fought over anything, hairdryers, curlers, the bathroom. They fought with an ugly hatred that frightened me and I couldn't figure out why. I hadn't raised my children to be angry at each other all the time.

"Debbie needed braces that October and had to have surgery on her mouth. She was in a lot of pain. Since we didn't have enough money, I took a second job cleaning the orthodontist's spacious home on Friday afternoons to pay for the braces. I'd come home exhausted on Friday nights. We still didn't have enough to make ends meet. The house was in a mess and I still had to cook supper.

"Larry's mother had sent us a few hundred dollars. Larry looked worn out from three job interviews that week. Debbie would be sitting like a lamb on his lap in the rocking chair and then, without warning, she flew to her feet, shouting and screaming at him with acid hatred. I threw up my hands.

" 'How can this be?' I pleaded. 'I'm working too hard to come home to this!'

"Larry was without a job for nearly three months but during this time he went out and bought a new car, without consulting me. He continued lifting weights and buying muscle magazines. He was usually too tired from working out to show any interest in romance or sex.

"Some time later he returned to the toy store and got a job as a stock clerk. He went down the ladder from manager to clerk. The pay was much less and I was discouraged!

"By now Debbie's anger was uncontrollable, and Trish was depressed. Christmas was coming and I worked myself crazy to make us happy. I baked hundreds of cookies and dozens of cakes. I did all that I knew to do.

"By spring I was fed up with this man, and the kids, and got into the car to just run away. I longed to simply get out from under it all, but couldn't just walk out. So I'd suck in my guts and stick it out.

"Often while Larry was at work, the kids and I would sit down and cry on each others' shoulders. I'd say, 'Well, we need to be thankful that you have such a good daddy. He's a preacher, he doesn't squander his money, just buys those crazy weights and stuff. Let's just thank God for such a good daddy and try and honor him.' Deep down inside I knew that I was lying.

"So many times the girls came to me and said, 'Mom, I hate Dad, why don't you divorce him?'

" 'I'm leaving just as soon as I'm old enough and I'll make a home for you and Trish,' Debbie promised time and time again.

"Trish was quieter but stated her hatred as well. She would burn his shirts when ironing them or drop his utensils on the floor when setting the table and instead of getting clean ones she would leave the dirty ones at his place.

"As a mother, I was convinced that we could put up with insanity but never considered sexual sin. That does not happen in a good, Christian, God-fearing family. That does not happen.

"A certain church in a small town needed a preacher. It was several hundred miles from Lincoln and Larry was invited to go to preach a trial sermon. I taught Sunday school and, in a way, it was good because it brought back memories. The people seemed to enjoy his preaching, although I found myself getting very uncomfortable listening to him. It wasn't the same. The presence of the Lord was not there. I was frightened. It all fell through, anyway.

"The girls were growing up and Debbie was giving me hell all of the time. Together the girls took a paper route but could agree on nothing. Larry ruled them with absolute authority and laid down all of the ground rules for their paper route as well as their personal lives. We lived such a closed and weird life. The girls were never allowed to stay overnight at a friend's house. They were allowed to do virtually nothing outside of the home except attend band practice. Everything was out of sync, but I put up with it to shut him up. I just could not handle another of his angry, hateful outbursts.

"Maybe once a year I'd get frustrated to the point of screaming and they'd all stand back, shocked, and say, 'What's the matter with her? Why is she so mad at us?' But it would clear the air. I'd apologize and we'd all go back to our kind of normalcy. We considered ourselves lucky if Larry didn't break something at least once a week, and if he didn't break something tangible, he never missed an opportunity to smash our hearts.

"If I asked Larry to help me discipline the girls, now ages 15 and 13, he'd cruelly abuse them. Once when Debbie was ugly to me, I told him. He beat her and she began screaming for mercy. I saw him viciously beat her breasts and stomach. I shouted at him to stop and he did. I was scared. I followed Debbie to her room and hugged her and promised, 'I'll never allow him to punch you again.' I could see the fear in her eyes and the hatred in his. I simply did not know what to do.

"One night after work I thought, 'Why not just drive off into the sunset?' But I reasoned, 'I can't leave him with the girls,' and I'd steer the car back home. Another time when the girls and I were out shopping, I thought, 'I'll just leave right now and never go back.' But I snapped myself back into reality because I wasn't a quitter!

"Then there was the night that Larry was late coming home from work and I thought, 'Maybe he was in an accident and died. Maybe they will call me from the hospital and it will be all over.' It sounded so good in my mind, but I felt guilty. I asked God to forgive me, but I wasn't really sorry. I was so upset, but would keep on going because it was required of me.

"Everything in the Bible teaches us about submission. Larry took it to extremes. I couldn't go to the grocery store unless he OK'd it. If I said, 'Look, I'm going to the grocery store, we're out of milk,' he'd say, 'Well, since you decided and I didn't, your decision is invalid. You can't go!' He was driving me insane. I didn't spend money indiscriminately. I saved for everything we bought and yet had to obtain permission three days in advance to be allowed to go to the store.

"In misery I would pray, 'Oh God, if you don't move in my life, I can't survive.'

"I spent a week fasting and praying, trying to assess the situation. 'What is wrong, God? Show me! Something has to be seriously wrong ... I can't make it right unless You do ... I can't live in this kinky way anymore, oppressed by this man and his unrealistic rules, having his authority suffocate us all. Do something now!' When I cried out my prayers just seemed to bounce back. But I persisted for the week and the burden of this situation almost crushed me.

"Then it lifted.

"One of the final blows came when Trish got a vaginal infection and didn't tell me about it for a long time. I had picked up the dirty clothes and noticed a thick, yellow discharge in her panties. I questioned her and she himmed and hawed and said, 'I traded clothes with my girlfriend.' I talked to one of the nurses in the office next to us and she said, 'Make sure they are not wearing their jeans too tightly.' I was convinced the reason for this ugly infection was wearing their friends' clothes. I went to the pharmacy and got a creme without needing a prescription because Larry refused to have the children seen by a doctor. I returned home and laid down the law. 'We'll wash your clothes in real hot water and use this new kind of soap.'

"Trish's private parts were inflamed and very sore. Two weeks later, Debbie got it and then I was also infected! During 17 years of marriage, I had never had an infection like it.

" 'No Compromise' became my theme song. The song was on one of my Christian music tapes and every time I heard it my heart would break because I knew that I was compromising with God. Every morning I'd wake up and have to gather all of my strength just to get out of bed. I knew that God expected my best and I just didn't have it to give. We didn't have a television, so I wasn't distracted that way. But I had spent hours in the library reading love stories. We were attending church, but not participating, just coasting along. We failed badly in our marriage and as parents. Larry was running me ragged and I had no time to read my Bible or pray. Just a glance at the Bible and prayer on the run was about all I managed. I worked 18 hours a day, cooked supper, cleaned the house and looked after a man who wouldn't even put gas in the car. He only cared for his weights. Then he showered and wanted his dinner at 8:30 p.m. He lived a life of luxury at our expense. Between him and the doctor's office I was wearing out. My allergies were killing me and I hardly had time to go to the bathroom. I encouraged Larry to listen to the song, 'No Compromise,' but he refused. Then I noticed that things were missing, several of my tapes, including 'No Compromise' had disappeared. When I asked if he had seen my tapes, he'd rant, 'I don't know where the heck your stuff is!' I didn't blame him. Somehow it would turn up one day.

"Summer was coming and I wasn't looking forward to it. Larry asked his mother to babysit the girls while we both worked in the daytime. I was furious. They didn't need babysitting, we were bringing a sick woman into our house and I had no say at all about it. Then Larry became more and more restrictive. The girls could not go swimming without his supervision and were not allowed to wear shorts. If boys were in the playground in our neighborhood, Debbie and Trish were not allowed outside. When he worked evenings, he'd call every 20 minutes and inquire, 'Are you watching the girls outside? What if they have a boy over?'

" 'So what?' I'd shout. 'I trust my girls. What's the big deal?'

"They knew the facts of life. They learned them back when they were children. They knew what was right and wrong. My girls didn't have any boyfriends and they called me if they needed anything.

"Larry was home three mornings a week and my sister Theresa lived a block up the street. She and her husband were welcome in our house anytime. Debbie and Trish had to be home to deliver papers at 5 o'clock, and I wasn't worried about them. I knew that they didn't like each other very much and that he stirred up competition between them. But I couldn't stop it because I couldn't stop the competition he was causing between us. There was a wall, a barrier between us that I was not even able to speak about. In 17 years he never heard what I said, never listened to me. I didn't realize what a good thing a two-way conversation was until I had a chance to visit and talk to two friends. But Larry would voice his opinion and we all just shut up. There was no discussion.

"Because Grandma Stella was coming, I decided to take an hour off from work and scrub the house top to bottom. Depression descended and settled in my mind as I cleaned. When Stella arrived she even took the liberty of changing our furniture around. She was the kind of woman who took over the kitchen and I couldn't so much as make a sandwich. In fact, I didn't even walk into the kitchen if she didn't walk out, because there wasn't room for the both of us. In a nutshell, she was nearly as difficult to put up with as her son!

"I had almost finished everything except the dusting, paying a few bills and buying the last-minute groceries. The one big job left was to move Debbie's bed to the basement, because Larry's mother was going to sleep in her room. Our basement was a mess, except for the area that Larry had fixed into his study and gym. His weights and books were the pride of his life and kept in perfect order. I'd tackle the basement tomorrow.

"I was hurrying to close up the office at 3 p.m. Three big bags of trash were waiting to be taken out. I picked them up and walked quickly through the outside door, when one of the bags hit the side of the door and slammed against my leg. The instant pain was like a deep sting which spread down my entire leg. I reached the garbage bin across the parking lot and my leg was trembling uncontrollably with pain when I put weight on my foot. I got the nurse in the doctor's office next door to look at it and she cleaned off the blood around a large bruise that had formed on my calf.

" 'Go home and rest,' she admonished. With still so much to do, I drove to the bank, borrowed money to pay up the miscellaneous bills, got the groceries and then headed to the park where the girls were practicing with the band for the coming Fourth of July parade. I propped my leg up on a chair until the children had finished. It ached but I refused to think about it.

"At home the girls started supper and I dragged myself upstairs. By now the pain was excruciating. I knew something was wrong, and put a heating pad on the bruised area. Larry arrived in a black mood and was furious that I was in bed. The house was untidy, and supper wasn't ready. But he just worked out on his weights.

" 'I'm sorry,' I said quietly from the bed, 'but I'm not getting out of this bed.' The girls fed him supper.

"In the middle of the night I had to go to the bathroom. For the first time in our marriage, that I can remember, I woke Larry up. I'd been sick before and I'd been hurt but I never woke the man up to help me out. I couldn't get out of bed. He got up with much stress and helped me to the bathroom. On the way out, unintentionally, he bumped my sore leg into the door frame when trying to turn me around. I fainted and fell to the floor. He was panic stricken when I came to and kept saying, 'Judi, what happened, what happened?' He dragged me back toward the bed and I leaned up against the side of the bed, still on the floor. Meanwhile, he got into bed and went soundly asleep.

The pastor looked at me in sheer disbelief.

"Saturday I was no better. I couldn't even sit up. By noon my head was swimming but I forced myself downstairs to eat lunch with Larry and the girls and give them some instructions of how to get things into a semblance of order for Grandma's arrival the next day. I returned to bed and cried. All I could hear was the girls fighting and Larry browbeating them, just as he had treated me for years and I just could not stand it.

"How could he be so debasing and treat them like they were subhuman? They were fine children and they did a good job and I was proud of them. But he just reamed them out! It hurt me so badly. I could not handle the abuse. When we were first married he hit me. But I soon learned how to avoid those situations. There was no way I was going to let my kids go through it. Over the years I had built up a protective shell and pulled myself inside. 'You only have to hurt so much,' I believed. But I was not going to let my children live with this.

"That night Larry took the girls to the big water slide. My leg continued to hurt and felt like something was stuck in it. When they returned home I said, 'Larry, you just have to take me to the doctor.

"We had discussed it before and he would not allow me to go to the doctor. I said 'Either you take me or I'll call the ambulance.' Well, he picked me up, took me to the car and drove me to the emergency room at Midlands Hospital. They examined me and said they didn't see anything wrong. I said 'It's killing me. Would you please x-ray it.'

"They did. The technician came out holding up the x-ray saying, 'I don't believe this! Man, will you look at this. There is a disposable needle, one and a half inches long, embedded in the calf muscle of her leg!'

"The doctor said, 'It doesn't seem too deep. Do you want me to try and get to it?'

"I said, 'Sure, if you don't take it out I don't know what I'm going to do.'

"He gave me a local anesthetic and got out his scalpel and began to cut. I almost fainted. Then the doctor said, 'I don't see it and don't want to go any deeper into the tissues because you don't have anesthetic that deep. I'll let the surgeon look at it.'

He sutured me up, and sent me home after giving me a medication for pain. I went to bed.

"The pain was waiting for me when I awoke in the morning. I called the hospital and asked to speak to the surgeon. He told me, 'You get right on over here. We have to see to that leg.' Larry had just enough time to take me back to the hospital and go on to the airport and pick up his mother.

"Sunday night my sister came and sat with me. The doctor checked me over and prepared me for surgery saying he had to go in and look for the needle and he would keep at it until he found it. I was so weak from the pain and domestic tension that I was about to collapse. I was given a surgical shave and scrub, my leg propped on a pillow. As the nurse put a sheet over me she said, 'I'm going to go and get you some medicine because you are the first in line for surgery. We'll get you out into the hall and wheel you on down to surgery at 5 a.m.' I tried to be brave but laid there and cried.

"It came to me almost in a flash, that I wasn't afraid of dying while under the general anesthetic. I'd been working for doctors over many years and was no fool. As a matter of fact, to die would have been a relief. But I was afraid that if I did die, my children would be stuck with their sick father. They didn't deserve him, and if I wasn't there to intercede, they wouldn't survive to adulthood. It hurt me so badly to realize that everything rested upon me. I knew that I was exaggerating but, at the time, it was so real. Every nerve in my body was raw. My spirit was naked and exposed. I had no covering and no comforter.

"When the Demerol started to work, I began to relax and asked God to take care of my children. I knew that I was a lousy mother and they had an insane father but what could I do? I'd taken care of him so long I felt like a mother with a little afflicted child. He was just my duty in life. But I was sick of my duty. I'd see it through to the end, even if it killed me. I was determined I would not let my children be destroyed by this man.

"I knew the only salvation they had was to grow up and leave home and get away from him. I couldn't leave but at least they could look forward to it someday. I said, 'God, don't let me die, I don't want my children to be stuck with him. I want them to be free someday even though I never will be.' I realized the bondage that we were in.

"I clearly saw that all the games the girls and I had played ... and all the, 'Don't tell Daddy that,' and 'Hurry up and find that before Daddy gets home,' and the, 'Don't move it because Daddy will be mad,' and 'Don't touch that, Daddy doesn't want it.' — all these ridiculous games were played to the best of our ability to protect our sanity. All we did was try to second-guess someone who was so unpredictable, whose fuse was so short. We didn't speak for fear we would set it off.

"My leg started to feel funny and if I turned a little, something scratched against the sheet. It was 4 a.m. I called the nurse and said, 'Would you please put a Band-Aid over where the stitches are so that I can get some rest? Every time I move the sheet it catches on these stitches.' She pulled back the covers and put a bandage on the stitches that were there and said, 'I'll be right back.' She returned with another nurse, and shone a flashlight on my leg, then left without saying a word and returned with the nurse in charge.

"The head nurse said, 'The scratching is not coming from your stitches, there is something sticking out of your leg!' I looked down and one half inch from where the stitches were was a needle sticking out of my leg.

" 'Evidently, when we gave you the Demerol, it relaxed you enough to allow this needle to make its way to the surface. I'm going to call the doctor,' the head nurse said.

" 'Hallelujah!' I silently shouted.

"She came back with a pair of tweezers and pulled the needle out. I just watched. There it was, tissue and blood clung to it, but she had the needle. I was so thrilled. She picked up the phone, cancelled the surgery and sent me down to x-ray. There was nothing in my leg. The next morning the doctors looked at the needle and looked at my leg and pronounced me well. I knew that God had worked a miracle.

"I phoned Larry and told him that I didn't have to have surgery and he was happy. I was weak and exhausted from the whole ordeal so they kept me in the hospital three more days. They treated me for possible infection and also for my allergies which limited the range of antibiotics that I could receive. Except for the exhaustion and severe damage to my muscle, I was in the best shape I'd been in for a long time. My sister Theresa was there every night. She brought me flowers, candy and magazines. She cared for me.

"I cried in self pity and said, 'Thank you Jesus for my sister because nobody else cares.' Larry visited me twice for half an hour. I didn't want to see him. I didn't care if he ever came. Theresa was there. She took me home and got me settled and faithfully came and checked on me every day after that for a week, while I got my strength back.

"Meanwhile my boss, Dr. Martin, was furious with me for being off work. He couldn't believe that I wasn't there when he needed me. He was a lot like Larry. About two weeks later, I returned to work, but my leg was still sore. That evening I decided to walk up to my sister's, just a block away, to get some exercise since the swelling had gone down. Larry and his mother were going to take a long walk around the neighborhood and the girls were roller-skating on the sidewalk. I started out the back door and they went out the front. Debbie saw me up the street and skated towards me, looked directly at me and said, 'Mother, I'm so sorry!'

"She collapsed, sobbing in my arms, and I just held her and said, 'Everything is going to be all right, don't worry about it, I'm fine.'

"She said, 'I didn't mean that,' and skated off. I really didn't fully understand what she was talking about.

"I was reduced to tears for the tender moments with Debbie were few and far between.

"Tension was building like a volcano ready to explode. Larry's mother said she was worn out being with us and playing nursemaid to me. After all, she had come for a holiday. The big July 4th weekend, which we had planned weeks in advance, turned out to be a dismal failure leaving the girls and me wild because of Larry's indecision and confusion. I pulled myself together and went to work on Tuesday. Larry took the girls swimming but when I came in, he and Debbie were in the middle of the worst explosion yet. I was mad at him for making her that incensed and disgusted with her for speaking so terribly to her father. I was exhausted with both of them.

"I thought,

" 'God, do something!

" 'I can't handle this strife!

" 'I wasn't raised in this kind of hell!

" 'I never functioned well in it, but I'm at the point where I *expect* it and I know that's *wrong!*

" 'Please have mercy on us!'

"I had no idea of the hell the girls were secretly experiencing. I took my medicine and went to bed early.

"Then ...

"It was 2 o'clock when Debbie came in and ..." My voice broke "... and told me about Stella stumbling onto her in the basement — with her father.

"My world blew apart, collapsing completely and totally.

"Larry could have shot the children dead and it wouldn't have hurt them as much. I love my children and will stand up for them," I confessed to the pastor.

Then I broke down and cried again.

"I don't know what to do ..."

I trembled with emotion. "But something has to be done."

As I cried, the pastor spoke with authority. "My wife is a social worker. Would you mind if I called her and told her your story?"

I nodded, believing that this was the only man who could help me at this precise moment. "Please tell me what to do," I wept.

"Go to work now," he said patiently. "I'll get in touch with a few people and I'll contact you and let you know what is happening. Give me your telephone numbers at home and work."

"Yes, sir," I said and thanked him for his time and care. I stopped in the bathroom on the way out to powder my red swollen eyes and replenish the lipstick I'd eaten off.

It did little good, for I sobbed all the way to the office.

I couldn't imagine how I would be able to face my second day of work with no sleep.

When I inserted the key into the lock, opening the door to the dental clinic, the phone was already ringing.

3

POLICE

"Good morning, this is the Dental Clinic." The lady on the line identified herself as Ruth Wilkes of Clark County Social Services.

"Could you hold?" I asked. The reception room was full of patients. I pressed the hold button and went back to an empty office to speak with her.

"I've just spoken to your pastor," she said, "and he has given me a synopsis of what's been going on in your home lately.

"It sounds as if you've been living in a pressure cooker."

"You're right," I said, "I think I'm overdone."

"I'm going to notify the police," she informed me.

"Would you?" I said.

"Definitely, are you willing to cooperate?"

"Yes, I am."

"Well, then I'll be back in touch with you soon."

Thank you." Click.

My knees were like jelly, and I sank to a nearby chair and prayed for strength before going back into the reception area. This was the beginning of the end of all that I had known of 17 years of marriage. I was terrified, but calmly relieved at the same time.

An hour later I was called by a police woman. "Good morning, Social Services called and I think that we can help you, if you will let us."

"Please do."

I was relieved. I who had spent years feeling trapped, hopeless, and defeated was speaking with someone who apparently was interested in helping me. "Could your children talk to the police?" she asked.

"Yes, they will," I replied.

"Very well then, I'll send an unmarked car with a detective to your home at 11 a.m."

"Thank you."

She hung up and I dialed home. Larry had left at 8:30 a.m. to work in the toy store.

"Hello, Stella ... this is Judi."

"Yes."

"Please put Debbie on the phone."

"Yes, Momma?" Debbie said.

"You and Trish get nicely dressed. A detective is coming to take you to the police station. Don't be frightened, they want to talk to you, it's going to be all right, will you be ready?"

"Yes, Momma."

"Fine." Then I added, "You go right ahead and tell them all about your daddy. Debbie, tell Trish to do the same." She agreed.

Some time later the police picked up the children and Larry's mother, and took them downtown to the police station.

Try as I might, I could not keep my mind on the office work, though it was pretty routine. At 11:30 a.m. the police woman called me again.

"I called you earlier from the police station. Your children are here with us making out a written report. I think it would be good if you came down here, too. Drive safely now, don't rush. We'll wait for you."

"Yes, I will, thank you."

My former world had crumbled around me, I was a bundle of nerves, my children were at the police station.

I knew I had to speak to the doctor so I took a deep breath and walked into the room where he was performing routine surgery.

I tiptoed towards him, gathering courage, and whispered, "I need to speak with you right now."

"Can it wait?" he grunted. I had broken his power of concentration and he was annoyed with me.

"No!" I was just as emphatic.

He stopped his surgical procedure with deliberate annoyance and came out into the hall.

I whispered, "Look, I've got to leave, and I probably won't be back. I'll see you tomorrow."

"Wait a minute, what's the matter?" Dr. Martin asked.

"My children are at the police station. We're having trouble with Larry."

"Are you sure you won't be able to get back today?" He hadn't perceived the agony of my situation.

"You're a fine lady," he lectured, "but that evidently doesn't matter for anything."

An atom bomb went off in my soul. He stepped back, blinking, sensing the explosion of pent-up rage.

"I'm sorry for the inconvenience, but I must leave!" I managed to get out, tucking my purse under my arm.

I left, closing the door slowly but firmly. Crying and praying, I finally arrived at the police station.

My girls and Stella were seated around a circular table in a conference type room. A lamp hung over the table bathing their faces in light. They looked white and sick.

The policewoman who had first called introduced me to the police chief, the detective and patrolman.

Debbie sat at one end of the table visibly upset, biting her nails. Papers and pencils lay in front of both girls. Trish, head down, introverted, sat next to her grandmother. Stella's posture was erect, her attitude hostile, exuding an air of complete superiority. I joined the unhappy trio and we were served coffee and doughnuts. My stomach, frozen with tension, refused the coffee. I pushed the Styrofoam cup away.

"Ma'am," the chief began. "We have finished the interviews with your children. He stood with the written results in his hands. Please look at these and tell us if you feel they have been truthful." He looked at each face around the table.

I read the reports before answering his question.

"To the best of my knowledge, I taught them not to lie and as far as I'm concerned, if they said it happened, it happened!" I told him.

"Your girls told us that your husband had a loaded shotgun in your bedroom," he interrogated. "Is that correct?"

"Yes sir," I whispered, meeting his intense, concerned gaze. "I know that if he finds out that we are here, I may not live through the night."

"I expect not!" It was the voice of the policewoman. Her countenance was cold but she seemed to care.

Detective Taylor, sitting next to me, leaned over with quiet authority, placed his hands on the papers the girls had written and said very distinctly so that it would sink into our exhausted and shocked minds, "We have all the evidence that we need just from what your daughters have written here."

About that time Ruth Wilkes, a social worker from the Juvenile Court, came into the room. The pastor's wife had called her earlier that morning. She had been the first to call me. It seemed like years ago.

She asked us to go over the details of exactly what had taken place in our family during the last two years. I was shocked and distressed by much of what the girls said, for it was the first time I was hearing the true story from them. I wanted to crawl under the table.

Instead, I leaned into the back of the chair, too weak to move. As I listened, I realized that this whole mess was now out of my hands, and I had to consent with what was going on even if I didn't understand.

Detective Taylor took me back to the house. He picked up the loaded shot gun which stood against the wall in our closet. I didn't know it at the time, but this marked the beginning of handing over many strange and telling possessions that my husband had kept.

Time dragged. Detective Taylor decided to keep us at the station until they picked Larry up at 5 p.m. as he was leaving his place of work. During the tense wait, Stella looked straight across the table at me, her eyes narrowed into slits. She spat the words out, "Judi, I told you not to marry him 17 years ago and look what you went and did! It's all your fault, because you didn't do what I said."

I couldn't believe it! Ruth Wilkes, the social worker, looked at me. I was tripping out — fighting tears and anger all at the same time. I bit my tongue. How could she be so self-righteous and vindictive at such a vulnerable moment in my life? I knew that she was unstable and changed her opinion on the spur of the moment. Even though I thought she had a valid point, this was not the time and place for such a discussion. She kept on needling me until the girls and I just had to leave the room.

Then she turned to the police and began to tell them why it was all my fault. I didn't know how to handle it. I'd never been to a police station before, and had only dealt with the police in a very superficial manner. Now here I was, surrounded, and our lives were literally in their hands.

The police chief made a statement that I was surprised to hear.

"You are the first woman in Clark County to report her husband for sexually abusing her children."

"I am?" I gasped, unbelieving. There was nothing special about me. Some "first," I thought to myself.

"Usually we get this kind of information through the schools," Ruth Wilkes explained. "A teacher will pick it up, or a student will say something to her best friend who in turn will go to a teacher. Once it is reported, then we can investigate."

I was flabbergasted to think that I was the first woman who had ever come to them and asked for help. I was shocked to think of the other mothers so blind and dumb, so caught up in the maze of sin and deception that they couldn't see. Yet, I mustn't judge. It had taken me years to get to this place.

Looking back, it is a gray blur. About 5:30 p.m. a call came through to the station — and I heard Larry's name. "This is Patrolman 372, we have in custody the suspect, apprehended in the underground tunnel at the crossroads in front of Milligan's World of Toys. We are now heading towards Lincoln Central Police Station."

Without a moment's hesitation, we were bundled into a car and driven home. My husband would enter the station soon, handcuffed. It was very hard to go home knowing that they had arrested Larry. On the other hand it was the easiest thing that I had done in years because the responsibility and burden for his well-being was off my shoulders. It was pure relief not to worry about, "What are we going to do with Daddy, or how are we going to make him happy when it's an impossible task." The decision was no longer mine and, thank God, I didn't have to make it anymore.

As we drove up to our duplex I realized in part that the girls and I were embarking upon a whole new way of life, and with it a dark spectrum of emotions. I look back now, after having lived through it, and must smile a little at the naiveté of my reassuring words, "Well, kids, everything is going to be fine." For a long time it wasn't.

The shock that we had all experienced seemed to keep us in a state of animated suspension. It was as though the focus of our life was off center, and we couldn't see any clear outlines. I went up the block to my sister Theresa's home and we talked and cried together.

As soon as Debbie stepped inside the door she ripped Larry's list of rules from the refrigerator. I remember the rules very well:

> *All activities okayed through me.*
> *Paper route only through me.*
> *Sunbathing at home only, and when I'm*
>   *home only.*
> *Tell me the exact route you take home*
>   *from school.*
> *Allowance to be paid when all chores are*
>   *done, if grades are reasonable, attitude*
>   *is good, papers delivered in*
>   *reasonable   time, collections made.*
> *Money can be spent with family*
>   *approval.*
> *No increase in activities,*
> *You will pay me for gas.*
> *This is your job, you do it!*
> *If not, heavy points off.*
> *Less play time!*
> *Family activities come first.*

As she crumpled the list of rules into a ball, she shouted, "Part of the problem was you. You just didn't care. You were too lonely and hurt to care about us. Remember how I told you to divorce him and you'd send me upstairs? Remember?"

"Yes, Debbie, I remember," I conceded, "I'm sorry."

I *was* sorry!

"Well, if you were so sorry," she accused, "Why didn't you do something? Trish and I were trapped here. We packed our bags several times to leave and Dad found out and would say, "If you run away they will send you back here and then I'll fix you."

"Yeah — he fixed us all right." Sarcastically Trish threw the words at me.

"Girls!" I screamed. "I'm sorry,"
I sobbed.

They stood back watching, almost savoring my torment before reaching out. Desperately we clung to each other in speechless silence.

We resumed the pathetic gesture of collecting Larry's sick notes from the bathroom mirror, our dresser and the kitchen. They carried identical admonitions, written to himself — "fix car tires," "shave beard," "resign from the ministry," — he had repeated himself over and over, never able to make a decision.

Somehow this little exercise of freedom felt good. We hustled around in the living room, changed the furniture around and put things the way we wanted them. I'm sure these were all symptoms of stress and we were its victims in desperate search of release.

We went through the routine of getting something on the table and ate, not even tasting the food. After supper, while the girls did the dishes, Stella sat me down and told me how much Larry resented her. I thought to myself, "Woman, if you had told me this 17 years ago, I'd never have gotten into this mess."

"He has always hated me, Judi," she confessed brokenly.

This was the same woman who a few hours previously was nailing me to the cross in the police station declaring that it was all my fault. I held my peace, I was just too tired. I could see that anyone who resents their mother has a hard time coping with a wife, or other women. Sadly, but clearly, my mind registered the fact that Larry hated me. But he hated himself more to vent such destruction upon the girls. Because I was his caretaker he had been very comfortable at my expense. I had unknowingly provided him with an outlet for his sexual perversions. I was unable to reach out and comfort Stella.

Instead, everything inside of my exhausted spirit and body silently screamed out to this pathetic woman, "Leave me alone!"

We went from one crises into another. No sooner had this conversation finished than Debbie insisted on taking me down to the basement. She had moved her bed into Trish's room and refused to ever stay down in the basement again.

She said, "Mom, when you were sick in the hospital, Auntie Theresa gave me this to read." She opened *The Reader's Digest* to an article exposing incest. "I've read it, Mother, and it tells all about the ugly things that people do with their children because they were abused in childhood. It says incest happens over and over again, it's an ugly recurring cycle. I read this last week for the very first time in my life. I realized then that Daddy had lied to me."

"What did he tell you, Debbie?" I gently questioned, inwardly bracing myself for the answer.

"He told Trish and me that you knew and approved of what he was doing with us and every daddy does that, and it was our duty to obey him."

"Debbie." I paused, weak and powerless in the face of this enemy that had come in and taken over, "You — you, do — believe me when I say I didn't know?"

My eyes searched her young but prematurely wise face.

She held my gaze and tears sprang up and coursed down her cheeks.

"I know it now, Mother," she whispered.

"Debbie, the proof that 'everybody doesn't do that' is the fact that your daddy is in jail." We clung onto each other and cried.

"Mother?"

"What, Debbie dear?"

"Did you know that he has a suitcase full of pornography?"

"No," I said quietly.

She led the way into his makeshift study and searched for something under the desk. She saw a briefcase, opened it and pulled out $80 in cash and then dozens of filthy magazines. She dug deeper into the side compartment and brought out two obscene pornographic books with vivid word descriptions, complete with diagrams of how to go about certain perverted sexual practices with children.

Silently, I reached over to the phone on his desk and dialed the number left us by the police. A police woman answered and I described what we had just found. She was at the house within minutes to collect this "evidence." The more we searched through the house, the worse it got.

It was very late by the time we were all ready to go to bed. Just as I was getting ready to go upstairs, Grandma Stella had backed both girls into a corner. Antagonistically, she pointed her finger at them accusing, "Why would you seduce your father? You're like Lot's daughters!

"In fact, you are *worse* — for you did it repeatedly!"

"What?" I shouted. "What do you think you are doing here?"

Turning around to face me, her eyes filled with hatred. The vitriol poured out,

"It is their fault, you know?"

"No, that's a lie!" I challenged. Adrenalin transformed my exhausted body into full battle alert for war. "While your precious son was having intercourse with Debbie, abusing Trish, pitting one child against the other and both of them against me, you have the gall to stand there and lay the blame on these two children? Who do you think you are? Go to your room and go immediately!"

I was too mad to sleep, so I called Theresa and related the conversation. She came over and went straight to Stella's room, knocked on the door and said, "Stella, you are going home in the morning, pack your bags."

"My reservations aren't until the end of this month," she said.

"Well, you are going home, and that's it. Get packed! I will personally take you to the airport in the morning." Stella came out of her room and called the airline about changing her reservations. I knew she was hurting. She was pathetic in her hatred against us and her blind devotion toward her son.

Crying, she hung up the receiver.

"I have a flight at 9 a.m."

I didn't even answer her.

The day had seemed to stretch into eternity. Sleep fled from my tired and frightened mind. I laid in bed stiff. Mentally I forced my muscles to relax into the supportive firmness of the bed. My mind worked like a giant computer, bringing up scenes from the past, flashing them onto the screen in vivid 3-D color. Helplessly I watched, the prisoner of my circumstances.

Larry's pleading face appeared and I sobbed until my entire body was racked with convulsions of soundless groans. Larry, how could he manage now, he needed me, how could I hurt him like this? I cried for him. Debbie and Trish flashed on the screen, their faces dark and angry, lashing out at me and each other and their father, uncontrollably.

The scene changed, screams filled my mind. Larry had Debbie by the hair, beating, cursing her. Then the screen filled with pictures of all kinds of sexual perversions, pictures I'd seen down in the basement in my own home. As though a wand was raised over me, my emotions of sorrow, remorse and self-condemnation hardened to fury, blinding hatred against the man who had damaged my girls.

I laid there in a prison of my past. The deepest hurt of all was to try to remember where I had gone wrong. I couldn't remember once ever saying, "No" to Larry, except when I had been camp cook the previous summer. I never caused a problem intentionally. I was superwoman, Johnny on the Spot. I couldn't count the number of glasses of water that Larry would wake me up in the middle of the night and demand I bring him. I denied him nothing, within reason, emotionally, spiritually or physically in bed. This bed that now seemed to smother and torment me.

The only mistake that seemed to press its way upon my already over-burdened soul was the fact that I had married Larry in the first place. Stella was right. Continually I had lied to the girls. When Larry caused a scene, I'd gather them and reassure them, "Your daddy doesn't smoke or drink, or run around with other women, and he's a preacher, honor him."

Now I was crying again. My face, neck and nightgown were soaked in salty tears and there was no end to the river. I just wish I'd known to tell them, "Don't you let him touch you!" I'd warned them to beware of strangers, not to take candy or to let people touch them in private places. But I never told them to be afraid of their daddy. I just wish I had known. I tried so hard. I don't know where I could have done better ..." I pulled the pillow over my head to stifle the sobs that once again racked my body, soul and spirit. I was undone. Loneliness and emptiness came over me like a cloud.

Maybe if I'd had an affair it would have been easier to forgive myself, or to justify myself, but I had worked so hard and did the very best that I could and still ended up a miserable failure rewarded with pain, heartache, brokenness and damaged children. I hoped that God heard my cries.

4

THE SURVIVORS

Larry had been arrested on Wednesday. When I came downstairs the following morning the girls were up and dressed and his mother was on her way out the door to the airport.

Detective Taylor had asked my permission to take the girls to the local hospital to be examined by a doctor. I agreed, but couldn't get permission to leave work and accompany them myself.

He arranged for a police woman to be with them all the time. Each child received complete physical and pelvic examinations including syphilis and pregnancy tests. Both girls were irritated with me that night for permitting them to go through such a demoralizing procedure.

As their mother, I was caught and torn because my first responsibility was to them. But my boss was furious with my long absence due to my recent illness and refused to allow me any time off. As much as I would have liked to tell him to drop on his head, I needed the job to keep food on our table. The girls were not able to appreciate this fact.

By Friday noon I was finally free from the longest week in my life. On Saturday the girls and I had an appointment with the doctor who had examined them the day before. We went to his office.

"Your daughters have suffered from extensive vaginal inflammation," he said, his words precise. "They have sustained severe muscle damage. The tissue breakdown is abnormal to children their ages. You understand they have received a wide scope of abuse."

I cringed, as he continued. "All we can do is to let time heal them and to clear up the infection."

Shame marked the three of us. Not even wanting to face the doctor, I silently nodded in agreement, too ashamed to speak because there was no self-justification.

Dutifully I got a prescription filled and every night at bedtime I inserted the antibiotic creme into the girls inflamed areas. For some reason, I could not understand, the girls absolutely refused to do this for themselves. In a way they seemed to be punishing me.

All medical reports were sent directly to Police Headquarters and Social Services. They became official documents that validated the written reports the girls had submitted, incriminating their father.

It was a heart-breaking, nasty business. Later the doctor gave a stronger antibiotic creme to combat what he termed as "non-specific vaginitis." The girls fussed and argued all the way to the doctor's appointments, and hated me for insisting that they get proper medical care. I understood that their sense of shame and anguish, and also helplessness, were afflictions even more severe than their young damaged bodies.

My mind returned back to March when I first noticed that Trish had a thick yellow discharge in her panties. That was four months earlier.

Frightened, alone, accused and condemned, my mind screamed, "How could you have missed the clues?" Their father systematically passed the infection to each of us as he diabolically possessed our beds and bodies. It was so sickening to have to face the truth. And I was part and parcel of their agony.

Trying to lighten the gloom and sense of personal defilement we all carried, we went out on a shopping spree, followed by supper and a movie. Larry absolutely forbade them to wear shorts. So we visited the biggest department store and chose bright stylish summer outfits. Waiting among the racks of clothes and mannequins, I began to experience a world that I had not even noticed before. Everything I saw offended me. Unconsciously, my mind categorized the fashions into "sexually exciting," "overexposure," or "seductive." No matter what came into my range of view, I saw it as sexually implicating. My world was turned upside down.

I guess we went overboard that first weekend without Larry. But what a relief it was not to have to beg him to be allowed out. We were free at last and went to the zoo and enjoyed three movies! However, no matter how busy we kept, our days always came to an end and once again we returned to the little townhouse filled with so much unhappiness and so many sordid memories. Each one of us was searching through the ruins of our lives. The question was: what were we looking for?

Finally I gathered courage to call my mother. It was painful. I cried before I dialed the number and I cried again on the phone. She wanted us to come home and I wanted to leave here so badly, but I couldn't. I knew that we were involved with lawyers and the court now and we couldn't leave.

My children were wards of the court!

After supper one Sunday night, Debbie gathered the family photo albums together into the middle of the sofa and began to pour over them. She called for Trish and me to join her. There were the pictures of when we had all of the foster children. Those were good times, well some of them were good.

"How did we end up moving into that backwoods town anyway?" Trish queried as she thumbed through the album. "Look, here's a photo of the big old parsonage. How many rooms did it have, was it 20?"

I relaxed between them with a cup of coffee and turned on the light behind us.

"Well, your dad tired of being an evangelist, and applied for a pastorate again and after some time we were given this church. The house was enormous because it had been a nursing home. Look, there's the river off to the left. Remember how swiftly it ran with icy water? The house was squeezed in between the church on one side and the cemetery on the other."

"I remember the day we moved in, it was fun running upstairs and down the long corridors and exploring all of the different rooms," Debbie exclaimed.

"Debbie and I shared a room," added Trish.

"It was that friendly social worker, Mr. Olsen, who helped us move in because we had agreed to take Junior," I interjected. "Remember? Look, here you both are, your first day of school. I was proud of the way you girls fit in so well and learned to make new friends quickly, real preacher's kids in that respect.

"Remember when Junior wanted to join the Air Force? He was 18 and had to pass an entrance test. Debbie, you were only 12 and helped him study and got better marks than he did on the practice papers. Poor Junior!"

While the girls leafed through several books, filled with pictures of them and our seven foster children, my mind replayed in perfect detail conversations Larry and I had engaged in. He forbade me to make value judgments, or decisions concerning the ministry.

One day a parishioner called and said, "Could your husband come over and visit me this week? I've been ill."

"Why, yes, of course, he can," I easily responded.

But when I related her request to Larry he was furious.

"No, I can't," he had bellowed.

"But why not, you're not doing anything, why can't you?" I had asked him.

"Well," he paused, thinking, "the reason I can't is because you said I could and I'm the one who makes the decisions, not you. If you decide, then I cancel the decision. That's the way it is!" He liked to preach but not to minister.

My mind ran on to the Christmas banquet especially for the Sunday School teachers. I enjoyed chatting and being a part of the community. In response to a question that one of the teachers asked me publicly, I told her what I thought.

All the way home Larry reviled, "Why don't you keep your big mouth shut? Who cares what you have to say, anyway?"

Numb with hurt, I had replied, "Larry, if you don't value my opinion more than that, then don't give me an opportunity to speak it. If you have appointments and dinners in the future you'll have to go alone, because I'm too busy."

He was frustrated at my ability to do things but he never could have functioned without me. I drove him everywhere as his poor sense of direction made it difficult for him to find his way home at night. Never again did I accompany him as the pastor's wife. Never again did he allow me an active part in the ministry. I had been willingly reduced to the rank of "driver."

My secret defense mechanism was to be busy. I refused to be intimidated and brow beaten because I had an opinion that differed from his. However, I lost the battle because I did succumb to hours of verbal abuse that flowed in a never ending stream.

"Remember Mary Sue?" Debbie's question broke my silent, negative train of thought.

"Yes I remember her well, another abused girl. She came to us when she was 13. I never told you girls that she had been molested by her brothers. That was one of the reasons why she was so angry and stubborn."

"I didn't know that!" Trish said, amazed.

"You didn't need to know it dear." I squeezed her hand reassuringly.

"Remember she ran away and the police and Mr. Olsen the social worker searched for a week before they found her with her dad," Debbie said. And then she was admitted to a mental hospital.

"Yes, I remember." I sighed wearily, finishing my coffee. "I knew she needed professional help, but we couldn't give it to her."

Debbie leaned over and looked up into my eyes. "Mom I don't hardly ever remember you hugging me. You were too busy looking after all the kids, reading or something else. When my period started, I was scared to death, even though you had explained it to Trish and me. I never got over how you just threw me a package of maxipads and that was it!" Her voice conveyed rejection.

"Debbie," I began, looking deeply into brown eyes brimming with tears, "will you forgive me?"

Her head nodded slightly as she bit her lower lip. "Yes," she whispered, "I'm trying to."

Trish put her finger on a photo of two ugly little girls and said, "Why did we ever take in those kids? They were weird, weren't they?"

"Well, Mr. Olsen called us," I explained, "and said, 'please take these two little sisters.' My first reaction was no, but I softened. They were four and six years old and came to us covered with chicken pox. Their names were Margie and Frances.

"I remember. I was so disappointed," Debbie reminisced, "because you said we were going to have two little sisters and they were so ugly!"

Again, my mind reflected on the stormy past and I remembered the night that I prepared the two little orphans — Margie and Frances — for bed. Larry made the rounds and prayed and kissed all the kids. That night he called me upstairs and there, standing in the middle of the bed, were both little girls with their night gowns up and their panties down saying in unison "We're ready!" Larry was so embarrassed he didn't know what to do. I was, too, but kissed them and tucked them in.

The next day while I was driving into town, Margie said "lots of men came and watched T.V. in my house while they waited for my mommie."

I asked Margie, "The man that came to your room, Margie, what did he look like?"

"He had a mustache, uh." She instantly realized that she had said too much and abruptly stopped. After that, Frances would make remarks to Larry that were out of place. At school she did everything backwards and seemed to have no ability to learn.

Debbie's voice brought me back.

"Margie was always having seizures," Debbie said. "Remember when we were picnicking and she had one in the lake?"

Debbie could be very motherly at times.

"The doctors said both sisters were mentally retarded, but the retardation was not due to birth defects," I explained.

Both Debbie and Trish became silent.

"They had been violently and repeatedly sexually abused which had resulted in extensive emotional damage," I explained. "This formed a blockage in their minds. As a result, they could not function normally because they had actually stopped thinking. These little girls boiled with anger directed at me because I was their adopted mother, so to speak. Especially, Margie hated her mother. If I ever tried to hug her, she went stiff as a board, and glared at me all the time. It took months for her to let me even hold her hand."

Both girls appeared astonished at what I was telling them.

"Remember," I pointed out, "it was you girls and Daddy who dressed her and got her to take her medicine because if I even spoke her name, she looked at me in fear, speechless. It hurts me to know that a woman can destroy her child like that," I said.

"Margie would say crazy things," said Trish. "Like one night at supper when we had spinach, she said, 'My mother makes me eat grass.' Why do people treat their kids so hatefully? Why do people? Why did you and Dad?"

Quietness settled down upon us and also a deep, deep sadness. I fought tears back and no one spoke but we each personally knew something of the dungeon that claimed Frances and Margie as prisoners.

Our hearts went out to the foster children, but here we were in an almost identical predicament of our own.

"There are no easy answers, Trish," I replied. "Parents many times are so sick themselves that they unintentionally afflict their children."

Through the lives of Mary Sue, Margie and Frances we saw how destructive the scars of sexual abuse are.

I was revolted to see their lives destroyed, handled so carelessly by selfish, unloving adults. They represent the millions of pathetic children who have been misused by adults, then discarded like empty cardboard boxes.

It was a pretty heavy conversation, yet I thought, maybe in the providence of the Lord, we were communicating through the tortured lives of the little people that we had actually opened our home and hearts to. The girls still had not been able to share with me any of the abuse they suffered from Larry personally. Perhaps, this evening together was a beginning.

"Look, here's Dwayne and Steve," Debbie said.

"They were nine and ten when they came to us, two little half-brothers with no home," I pointed out. "They had been caught shoplifting, but fitted into our family and were typical boys full of enthusiasm for life."

"Look, remember when Daisy came with all of the eye shadow and stuff?" Debbie asked. "I was really impressed because we were the same age! But I wasn't allowed to wear any makeup then. I thought she was so mature!" She chuckled to herself.

"Daisy was fully developed at age 12 and hated women and especially mothers," I explained. "Mr. Olsen said she had been abused physically by her mother and sexually molested by her father. The poor kid didn't know if she was coming or going. Remember how she'd break so many dishes when she got mad? I never thought I'd be able to handle that girl, but you know the Lord put a love in my heart for her, too."

"Come on, lets keep moving," Trish interrupted. "Who was this guy?"

"That's Ronnie," I answered. "He was 18 years old but, because of retardation, he was actually only six years old mentally. The doctors think the damage occurred when he was little, because his father tied him up to a tree and beat him. He was severely damaged, they said."

"All I remember is that he had a violent temper," Debbie added. "We never got along."

"Why did we have so many weird kids?" Trish demanded.

"Well Trish, first it was your dad's idea because he loved kids and we got $150 a month for each child depending upon their needs," I replied. "Daddy said the more the merrier.

"Besides it helped us get ahead financially. I took them because he told me to. But I did my best for them and took them on as my personal ministry for the Lord."

Then I changed the subject. "That boy under the oak tree with the ball is Robert. He came to us straight from juvenile court. But he was a reasonable boy. He used to talk to his mother long distance and then go to bed and cry, 'I want my mother.' He was sick with longing for her and his brother. He cried like a three-year-old and he was 14."

"Sure, I remember Robert," Debbie said. "He was the most fantastic storyteller. Remember how we'd all sit around the table and he'd keep us enthralled for hours?"

"Well, he was a great babysitter, too," I said. "So willing to help me with the little ones. I appreciated him. He couldn't concentrate at school though because of the fantasy and tall tales that filled his head."

"Dad was different then," Debbie said, almost wistfully. "Remember how he'd take us all hiking together. We'd carry the little kids on our backs. They slowed us down but nobody was left out."

"That's right, your dad thought it was heaven having a bunch of kids around and lots of places to go!" I answered.

"Oh look, there's Robert in his beautiful new suit that we all saved up for and bought him! He was so proud he marched around like a peacock," Trish said, jubilantly.

"Yes, that was a great Christmas," I said. "God was real good to all of us and we were beginning to function like one big family."

Turning to the next page, Debbie said, "Oh, here's Dwayne. Remember Mom?"

Yeah, I remembered.

The Juvenile Detention Hall had called while I was out, and the kids were in an uproar. Someone new was coming and they thought a new kid would break up their party. They had made a production of putting on plays, including dramas and comedies. Under Robert's direction they created a band and played popular songs as well as choruses. They never missed television. Now with a new kid they thought this fun would change.

Mr. Olsen and I had worked out the arrangements to go and pick up the new boy. We chose a Wednesday afternoon, a church night, so our gang got all dressed up and came along. We decided to go to McDonald's for a rare treat, and then have a few minutes to shop before evening service.

Mr. Olsen introduced Larry and me to the skinny, pathetic child with large brown eyes. He looked like a skinned rat.

"He has quite a medical report," the social worker had explained, "because he was born without a rectum and spent most of his life in hospitals. As a result, he grew up without parental supervision or discipline. Finally his parents gave him up as uncontrollable because he was so destructive."

Meanwhile, during our briefing, the tiny hellion we were discussing was swaggering around the other kids, acting like a big shot. He grabbed a coke bottle and gleefully dropped it from the second-story window, giggling loudly when it smashed on the pavement below.

"Dwayne, come over here," I commanded, grabbing him by the arm. Together we faced Mr. Olsen. Pretty soon I felt this tiny little guy next to me getting closer every minute. Before long his bony arms were around me.

"Dwayne can't write his name, and he'll need special education at school," the social worker said as he looked over the rims of his wide frames to see if I realized what a task I had on my hands.

I did and was taking notes as fast as he dished out the information.

Dwayne hung onto me as we left the building and headed for the car.

I noticed that he looked ratty in comparison to our other children who were dressed up.

"Wait," I said to Larry. "I'll change him before we get started."

We opened his suitcase out on the trunk of the car. The contents smelled like someone had gone to the bathroom right inside the suitcase. Everything was filthy! We ran into the local shopping mall and quickly bought him an outfit to fit a four-year-old. That night he sat on my lap throughout the entire church service and refused to budge. He curled up like a baby and fell sound asleep. When we got home, Larry carried him upstairs and tucked him into his new bed. Together we made the rounds to our very large brood and gained some sense of fulfillment knowing that we were helping each child to believe and have hope in the God of heaven who loved them. We loved, accepted, and did our best for each one.

The next morning, we took Dwayne to school and enrolled him in the special education class. The little fellow started to perk right up. The principal and teachers knew us because of Margie and Frances and, knowingly commented, "Oh, another one of your kids!"

I.Q. tests showed that he was a genius. The fact is Dwayne learned very quickly to read and write. He could take anything apart and put it back together. He worked very well with his classmates and they seemed to love him. He had endearing ways. But when he got mad, Mr. Olsen warned, he was destructive. His favorite saying was, "Nobody can handle me!" Because he was perky and chirped happily we decided to nickname Dwayne, "Cricket."

Accidents plagued our new boy. He'd back into walls to keep me from seeing his dirty pants.

"Can't help it," Cricket would implore. With his medical history I believed him and took him to see our family doctor.

"Rectal muscles have good control," the doctor said, examining Cricket on the table.

While palpatating his abdomen, he added, "What do we have here, a large fecal mass. This is his problem. This child is impacted."

We returned home with instructions along with rectal suppositories and an enema kit. While the other kids were still in school, Cricket and I went to work. I laid him on top of the washing machine in the bathroom. We labored for hours and the air was foul but Cricket got cleaned out.

He had settled in nicely when Mr. Olsen brought a box of his clothes and toys from home. I was grateful for the clothes as he had put on weight and was growing out of his old things.

Mr. Olsen warned me about a couple of things.

"I think you should know that this child has a history of running away, and has a tendency to light forest fires."

"Great," I thought to myself.

"Also, I want you to know, that when I read his police report, I thought he was 18 not seven. At age five he held up a grocery store with an armed pistol because he'd seen it on TV and it looked like fun. If you have any trouble, just give me a call!"

"Thank you sir, I surely will," I said, smiling at him. "We're believing for a miracle of healing in each one of these children. With God nothing is impossible!"

"Well, we'll see," was all he could concede.

After supper together we unpacked his box and there was a letter from home. "Cricket," I said, "there's a letter here from your mother."

"Oh." His voice got soft. "Please read it to me."

I sat down in the rocker and he climbed up into my lap. I began:

"Dear Dwayne:

"I want you to come home. You will understand how much I love and miss you. Your daddy has left us and your brother and sister are in other homes now, too. Remember Petie our little white dog? Well, he is still with me, and is my friend. Son, I

hope to see you someday, but I know that you can't come home just now. Remember that I always love you.

"Your Momma"

It was a hopeless letter and why the social worker ever let him have it I'll never know. Here I had a seven-year-old criminal in my lap who loved his mother and she loved him. But he'd never see her again. He had been eternally separated from his brother and sister and dog. He longed for them all. A terrible, almost fatal wound had been opened.

Cricket sobbed, "I want my mother, I want my mother."

I held him very tightly and said, "I want you to have her, too, Cricket."

"I want to see Petie," he wailed.

I'd never felt anyone else's pain as deeply as I did Cricket's that night. We cried together and he hung onto me and wouldn't let go.

Larry was away at a two-day church conference when Cricket, who was a good big brother, came running in panting after school.

"Cricket's gone!" he blurted out, cheeks aflame with excitement.

The kids all ran to the river to look for him but found no sight of him, only the swiftly flowing water.

I got into the car and drove down the road. There he was, marching along, dressed in Debbie's boots, Trish's sweat shirt and Robert's hat. I picked him up. He kicked and squealed. I spanked him right there.

He looked me square in the eye and shouted, "You can't handle me, nobody can!"

Just a few days later I got a call from school. He had been picked up walking away from school, up the main highway leading out of town.

Quickly I drove to school and there he sat with defiance written all over his face. A furious teacher, and perturbed principal greeted me.

"We're sorry, but this child cannot return to this school!"

I pleaded with them to give Cricket one more chance. I explained that if we couldn't keep him, he would be returned to an institution.

"All right, one more chance," the principal gravely ascented to my plea.

Apparently Cricket had stolen an eraser from another student and the teacher found it in his pocket. To keep from being punished he ran away.

Cricket and I returned home and sat on the front veranda. He put his head on his knees and cried. He was sorry.

After supper and homework, the boys were all together in the back room playing and the girls were amusing themselves upstairs. Cricket sat in the living room all by himself. I made a point of walking by and hugging him.

"You're doing just fine!" I encouraged.

By bedtime his heart was in his eyes. I sat down and said, "Cricket, I just don't know what to do."

He climbed up into my lap and started to cry. I started to cry, too, because it had been a hard evening for me. If I couldn't discipline this child we would not be able to keep him. I had prayed much for Cricket and it seemed God wasn't getting a miracle to us fast enough, although I knew he was never late.

"Momma, I'm sorry I ran away."

"I know that you're sorry, Cricket!"

"Momma, you can handle me now," he said, gulping between sobs, his little hand wiggled right down inside of my big one.

"I knew I could all along Cricket, but I just needed you to know it." After that we dried our tears and hugged and I put him to bed. He didn't run away again.

"Don't stop, Mom." Trish snuggled closer. "Tell us the rest of the story about Cricket."

"Well," I went on, "after you left for school I called Mr. Olsen to give him a report about Cricket. He was glad to hear he was doing better. His teacher also noticed that Cricket had changed.

"All of us were thrilled with Cricket's progress after that. Your daddy was wonderful to play and hike with you kids. When he was out in the hills with the kids you were all so happy. Meanwhile I was grateful to be home alone to enjoy a little peace and quiet."

Silently I recalled, in a flash, how he got angry because I didn't join in or participate. On the one hand he never lifted a finger to help me with the children, and he always expected a hot dinner on the table when they arrived back home. But in his own way he was reaching out to me, and I was refusing him. Sadly I saw it and was momentarily sorry.

Just to maintain that household was a full time responsibility. The kids kept me too busy to attend every church meeting and from going places with Larry. I also confessed to myself that I had used them as an escape from him. He wasn't happy because I wasn't what he wanted. I was so far from his definition of "perfect."

As the school year drew to a close, all of our kids had made good progress.

"Debbie, you girls did very well and were loving all of the commotion and just having a good time growing up," I recalled. "Robert really did well and actually was turning from an introvert into quite a sunshiny person. Daisy and I were working things out between us and communicating. And Cricket and Steve were good little brothers, functioning normally. Cricket was developing and growing up into a cute little boy. He still had some stomach trouble, but as long as I kept him on a good schedule, eating properly, and his bowels straight, there was no problem. I loved it."

Then I remembered summer camp where I was the cook. The children and I were making big plans to have a wonderful time, excited at the prospect of living in log cabins beside a lake. What a perfect escape from the confines of the parsonage and our little town that thrived on local gossip. Our brood had attracted a lot of attention being on display 24-hours a day, seven days a week. I was ready for a change.

It took several trips in both cars to get all of us and our luggage transferred to camp but it was worth it. We were going to have the summer of a life time. We got all the kids settled into their bunks and unpacked while Larry and I went back home for the final load. It was then that he turned on me with a wicked hatred.

"Judi, you have the best way of working everything for yourself. I don't want you up there all summer."

"But you agreed to it!" I was not going to be deprived of a great summer.

"Okay, okay," he steamed. "But Debbie and Trish have to spend every other week with me."

We drove into the camp grounds in the mid-afternoon and the kids came hooting and hollering to greet us. They were barefoot and full of fun.

Larry insisted that Debbie and Trish pack up everything and go back home with him. A disgusting scene followed.

Debbie turned the page of the album and there, smiling up at us, was Larry's face, surrounded by unhappy youngsters and a disgruntled wife. A camper had come up at that moment and snapped a picture and gave it to us later. I had pasted it into the album.

"Give me this picture," Debbie yelled as she tore back the plastic and snatched the five-by-seven colored photo out of the album. She leapt from the couch, opened the drawer of the end table, grabbed a pair of sewing scissors and began stabbing her father's smiling face.

"I hate you, I hate you, I hate you," she screamed, jabbing the picture, then tearing it into tiny bits. "Oh God," she groaned, sinking to her knees on the carpet, "your face will never be seen next to mine again, never, you hurt me so badly."

Sobbing, she curled up into the fetal position, arms around her knees. "Hurt so badly," she repeated between sobs.

Trish and I, outside of Debbie's circle of pain, watched, helpless to reach in and release its grip upon her. Wanting to be close, we knelt down to the carpet and wept with her.

Debbie laid there until the crying subsided. Silence enveloped us. We weren't at peace. Perhaps it was the feeling that the truth was finally coming out. My girls' rotten, sour secret was no longer a deadly secret of hatred, too crushing to bare another moment.

"Momma," Debbie said with a sadness in her eyes, "it all started to happen that weekend when Trish and I were forced to return to the parsonage with him, and you kept the other kids at camp. That summer he started to fool around with us when we were alone."

"He would say like, 'Come upstairs, we'll play a game together.' "

She then explained that he also separated her and Trish into different rooms.

Trish picked up on the details.

" 'Take down your pants,' he would demand. I saw that his face had shriveled up mean and tight. He barked again 'take down your pants.' Next he undid his zipper."

"I closed my eyes," Debbie said. "I wanted to go back to you Momma and camp but he just kept on bothering us."

Debbie began to scream, "I can't stand it any more. The way he torments me!"

Trish told me he made them run around naked.

"We had to sleep with him," Debbie added.

She clung to me sobbing, "I hate him."

I held her in my arms as if she were a two-year-old child.

Trish, the quiet one, was just as upset, but just wept silently.

I put my other arm around her and drew her close. My girls were 10 and 12 years old when this abuse began.

It was past midnight when I put them to bed. I had a time of special prayer with each one asking, beseeching the Father in Jesus' name to come into our agony with his loving, forgiving, healing power. We needed a miracle.

Both children were scarred from years of obscene sexual abuse. That night, opening the photo album had lifted the lid giving me a peek into their foul, dark world of supposedly innocent pre-teen years.

The girls began to doze restlessly. I stayed with one and then the other until I was sure they were sound asleep.

But sleep escaped me. I felt like a sentinel upon his watchtower. The enemy would not conquer us again.

No matter how strong my resolve, my heart continued to condemn me.

"How can I think so foolishly?" I asked myself. "The enemy has already been in to rob and destroy."

I put on the coffee pot and waited idly for it to brew, then returned to the living room, the photo albums and ugly memories. A sinister inner voice kept tormenting me by asking, "How could you be so blind?"

Quite honestly, my mind responded weakly, "I don't know, I'm not making excuses. It's the truth as far as I know it. I had never suspected my husband of this!"

I reopened the albums. Smiling faces of tanned and contented children looked up at me. Each one was desperately in search of the innocent childhood that had been so cruelly snatched away in dozens of twisted, wicked ways.

"No wonder Larry was so angry when he came up to camp on weekends," I thought. "He tried to destroy us because that was what he was doing to himself and his girls."

I wondered if his anger was a cry for help because he had begun to molest his children and couldn't stop himself? Then all hell broke loose. It just seemed that the old devil was out to destroy us all.

I remembered that during camp that summer Robert, who had been such a help and inspiration, began to whisper to the kids, "Momma is slipping out of her cabin at night and goes to the woods with one of the counsellors to do wrong things."

I told Larry about it when he came up that weekend and, to my horror, he sided with Robert, thinking he might be right.

I was furious and called Mr. Olsen who came and took Robert back to the Social Welfare Agency.

Then poor Cricket began to have troubles so I sent him home for a week with Larry and the girls. He returned, beside himself with agitation and hyperactivity. Daisy was the next to fall apart. The hatred that seethed in her heart now targeted me for open attack. I was in the middle of a crossfire of hatred between Daisy and Larry and got wounded. Finally, I gave in and called Mr. Olsen.

"Could Daisy spend a week with her grandmother?" I asked. He agreed and we never saw Daisy again.

Larry dealt me a blow by announcing that he was closing up the parsonage and going down to the coast to spend two weeks at the beach, his first real holiday in years. I was speechless. The next day Cricket hit a hornet's nest and several children were badly stung. I had to spank him and it was hard on us both.

I laid down in my camp bed exhausted, crying and praying. A crushing burden of prayer and intercession came upon me. My father had been a minister from my birth and had led me into the Baptism of the Holy Spirit with praying in other tongues from a tender age.

My mother, a warm, loving soul bathed our lives in prayer and intercession. I learned to serve others by watching her selfless example.

Since childhood I had invited Jesus to live in my heart and I knew how to apply His power over us all. No one needed to tell me that prayer was also praise and adoration to the Father which flowed into worship. Joy and exuberance were part of prayer because of "Immanuel," God with us.

During the years of my marriage I prayed daily in the spirit as naturally as drawing my next breath. Many times I didn't know how to pray as I ought and the Spirit of God would intercede through me, searching out the deep and hidden things, speaking mysteries to God.

Tonight was one of those times. Pressures were pushing at me from all sides. The lives of my children were at stake. My husband was no longer reachable — but God was.

Silently I called, "Oh my Father are you there?"

God spoke to me that night. He said, "Take your hands off, trust me, I'll work."

Those words calmed me as nothing else could. I fell into a deep, restful sleep. Only the Lord knew the shock awaiting me the next day.

At breakfast there was no sign of Cricket. He was gone for two days when finally a nearby farmer reported him. Cricket had started a fire that was now raging though the forest, out of control. That old, defiant "nobody can handle me" look was back on his face when he returned.

"Cricket, why did you do this?" I asked.

"I did it because I wanted to," he said. I sensed that something had snapped in him. I didn't know what to do.

The next day he ran away again. One of the counselors found him hiding in the woods. I realized then that I had lost control over him and, as much as I loved him, I knew that I could not cope with this rebellion alone.

It broke my heart to take him back to Mr. Olsen because I loved him like my very own. I was literally a mother bereaved of her children. I had lost three in the first weeks of camp. That night I could see that I had lost my husband, and innocent daughters. No wonder I was so burdened in prayer just before it all broke loose.

Camp was filled with good times, congenial friends, Bible classes, lots of help in the kitchen, camp fires, singing — all in all a blessed time.

By late August, Debbie, Trish, Cricket and Steve and I looked forward to going home and getting into the fall program. I was still fearful about living with Larry. He had become a different person that summer.

Everything was breaking down. The children felt the tension between Larry and me. As a result, Cricket and Steve, both teenagers, wet their beds every night.

Our fifteenth wedding anniversary came and went and all I could think of was, "How have I endured it this long?"

Another little voice way down inside persistently whispered, "Work harder, work harder."

And I did!

Larry came in after Bible study one evening and announced, "I have just given the elders my resignation."

I was bowled over.

"But the kids have just started school," I protested. I'd seen him quit over the years and I was sick of a quitter and it showed! "What are you going to do?"

"Oh, we'll move close to Mother and I'll get a job."

Shortly afterwards my sister Theresa called from Nebraska and, when she heard of Larry's decision, said, "We live in a nice new development. There's a townhouse up the street. I'll get an application and send it to you."

Larry wasn't enthused. He had hoped to return to New Jersey. However, when he called his mother asking for money, for the first time in his life she refused him.

Surprised, he hung up, and said, "Well, if she doesn't want me, we'll go to Nebraska."

Our long journey west had begun. Social Services did not want us to give up Cricket and Steve, as they had blossomed under our care. But I was struggling to keep afloat myself those days. The boys were returned to the care of the juvenile court.

That unseen voice continued to point out my mistakes. "You failed the children. You failed your husband and your own girls. You failed yourself and your God."

At 4 a.m. the telephone rang.

"Who on earth would be calling at this hour?" I wondered.

I picked up the phone and instantly I knew the voice of Larry's mother, Stella, crying.

"What is it, Stella?" I asked.

"The same day that I found Larry and Debbie," she whined, "Larry's brother Danny was in a terrible accident and is still on the critical list. They had to amputate one of his legs and most of his body is crushed. But ..."

She broke down and sobbed, fought to regain control and went on.

"But no one called to inform me. He forbade it. He hates me so much and doesn't want me around. He is furious with you for sending me home."

Isn't it curious, I thought to myself, that this hatred has festered almost a generation in Stella's sons, now grown men.

The subterranean hatred instilled by Stella and her husband is surfacing in our generation, twisted and poisonous, clothed in different expressions. Like a thunderbolt it had hit me and my children.

This knowledge brought me right back to the Ten Commandments, and a clarity of understanding.

I remembered the words from the Bible:

"I, the Lord thy God, am a jealous God visiting the iniquity of the fathers upon the children unto the third and fourth genera-tion of them that hate me."

The same scripture also admonishes us:

"Honor thy father and thy mother, that thy days may be long upon the land which the Lord thy God giveth thee."

There it was, three generations of hatred, now four! God's Word is true. Hatred in Larry's grandfather ruined Larry's father, who in turn twisted Larry, who molested his daughters. We were the fourth generation defiled by hatred. The scripture says we hate God first and it must follow through that man then unleashes this hatred against God's creation, himself and then out towards those he had a part in creating — his offspring.

I could hear Stella crying on the other end of the line. As much as I pitied her, I was unable to strengthen or even encourage, for I was only barely a survivor myself.

JUVENILE COURT

There was no bottom to the grief! Time and again I found myself drawn down to the basement to search through Larry's study.

He often hid money — and the overdue bills were piling up.

I had high hopes of finding some more cash tucked away. Shuffling through the papers on his desk, I came across the resignation he had written to the church which had licensed him as a preacher. It had been written three months previously, but he could never make the decision to sign it and send it.

Without a moment's hesitation, I dated it, stuffed it into an addressed envelope and mailed it.

Larry had been in jail four days.

Under his desk pad I found a letter addressed to Debbie which read:

Dear Debbie,

You are soon going to be old enough to date, and these are the rules that you will abide by:

1. *You will bring the boy home, and I will check him out.*
2. *I want to see his car and his driver's license.*
3. *You may begin your date at 7 p.m. and be back in the house at 10 p.m.*
4. *If you ever become pregnant, it will be your responsibility entirely. I accept no responsibility for you.*

If you fail to obey there will be severe repercussions. Sign here _____.

A bound journal also caught my eye. He had used it as a diary. Dates were recorded with times and places of outings he had made with the girls — to the zoo or swimming. It seemed innocent enough. I continued to flip through the pages, and there in the middle, I stopped because strange half-words with codes and brackets covered several pages. I paused, and looked closer.

"What is this?" I wondered, as I sat there trying to decipher the code. I believe that the Holy Spirit revealed that my hands held details, minute details, all dated in chronological order, of the obscene and vile acts that he had performed upon his daughters.

Without a moment's hesitation, I reached for the telephone on his desk and called the police. They had become my protectors.

While waiting for them to arrive and collect the evidence, I found another relevant paper. It was a plea: "My mind is blank, I don't know if I can cope and go on anymore. I'm tired of life, all it seems is a spiral downwards. I don't know why I even continue to breathe. Life has been so hard and things never seem to work out. All I do is exist. My mind just stays blank and I don't know how I'll ever be able to live any longer."

Larry had described his mental condition. After reading it, the police officer said, "This certainly makes him a candidate for the mental hospital. Don't you think it would be a good idea if we came and made a thorough search of your home, to gather up any remaining incriminating evidence once and for all?"

"Yes sir," I responded meekly. "Please do, and I don't want to know what you find." The evidence that I had found only drove the hurt deeper into my already fractured heart.

The search warrant for our home was signed by a county judge. It stated for all to read:

"On July 8th, the subject was arrested by the Lincoln Police Department on two counts of incest. From previous investigation we have found the accusations of Judi, Debbie and Patricia to be truthful. They have given to this department, some diaries containing evidence and to prevent destruction of further evidence, we are requesting this search warrant."

While several officers made a thorough search, the phone rang. "Judi, it's Dean and Carol, how are you all?"

They were old family friends. My heart began to beat furiously.

"You were on our minds constantly these past days, and we've been praying for you. Everything is all right isn't it?" Dean asked.

"Oh Dean!" I forced myself to reply. "Praise the Lord!"

Then, I lied. "Why, we're doing just great. Everything is in good shape out here. Thanks for calling though. It was real nice of you. Bye now!"

I hung up, devastated. How could I tell my friends that Larry was in jail, our world destroyed. I sobbed, asking God to forgive my lie, but I just couldn't tell the truth — yet.

Our king-size bed was the next thing to go. We threw it out into the garbage pickup area and bought a feminine single model. As far as I was concerned, Larry was not coming home. There would be no place for him.

One day he called from jail crying.

"Judi, you have to get me out of here."

He threatened suicide and begged me to bring him home. But I had already decided that I would file for divorce. I could not let him get close to the girls.

"I didn't put you in there," I thought. My desire to cope was gone.

He'd cry and say, "But they leave the light on here 24 hours a day, and I'm in this cell with all of these mean people."

"Listen, Judi," he pleaded, "I've been reading all this stuff by Chaplain Ray, and God has really been ministering to me. I've been asking him to forgive me." Chaplain Ray is a well-known minister to prisoners.

"Well," I replied, "Why don't you ask me for forgiveness?"

"But —" he was surprised, "I didn't do anything to hurt you."

"Oh you didn't?"

He cried and begged me to get him out of jail and bring him home. I knew that I couldn't. Fear of having to live through anymore phone calls forced me to get an unlisted number.

Somewhere in the blur of shock I went to his closet and emptied it of his clothes which took up the whole area. My things were crammed into the girls' closets downstairs. I put everything into boxes and carried them down to the basement, to sit beside his weights. I was determined not to look back. I was not going to be like Lot's wife!

I received a letter from the Juvenile Court, Clark County, Nebraska, naming me the custodian of our children, and with it came a summons for the girls and me to appear in court for the hearing. A lawyer was appointed for the children's interests as minors because they were unable legally to guard and protect themselves. The court also appointed a lawyer for me. Standing on the threshold of a world I knew absolutely nothing about, I was fearful. But God had promised if I took my hands off, He would work for us.

The county sheriff called to say, "After extensive testing, your husband will be admitted to the regional state hospital."

I had not expected this and I guess my voice mirrored my shock, "What is the diagnosis sir?" I asked.

"He is diagnosed as having —"

"Wait a minute," I interrupted, "let me get a paper and pencil."

"Are you ready?"

"Yes sir."

The sheriff continued, "He is diagnosed as having a passive dependent personality disorder with multiple psychosis."

"What about the original charge of child abuse?"

"Well, the charge is stated legally as 'sexual atrocities' for a duration of the last two years which contributed to the lack and decline of the two minors."

"Could you tell me one more thing sheriff?" I asked, gathering courage. "Please tell me, did he ever admit to doing anything wrong?"

"He did admit to some things. We have the statement he gave us the night he was arrested when he told one of our officers that he had been sexually assaulting his children for the two years. We also have the written reports of the children and their medical examination."

"Thank you sir, goodbye."

The situation was more serious than I expected.

Physically unable to get up out of the chair for a few minutes, I sat in shock until strength returned.

A short time later, a policeman called and asked me to bring four sets of pants, socks, underwear and shirts.

"Don't send nice things," he advised. "He'll probably not see them again as he will be in the state mental hospital for the next six to 12 months."

Dutifully I returned to the basement and packed a small bag.

I called Rob, my sister Theresa's husband, and asked him to accompany me to the police station, because I suspected I would have to speak to Larry. I knew that I'd be nervous and didn't want to drive home alone.

At the police station I was personally escorted by an armed officer into a small room. This room was different from any other that I had seen at the station.

It was cut in half by a glass panel.

I was given a chair and a telephone to talk into. Larry's face appeared through the glass on the other side of the room.

Instead of seeing a monster who had tormented me night and day, my eyes witnessed a nervous, pathetic man — my husband. It was difficult to superimpose the descriptions in his diaries on this gray stencil of a man.

He picked up his phone.

Leaning against the glass he looked at me with those big puppy-dog eyes and said, "Judi, you have to get me out of here. Give me a chance to come home and everything will be fine."

His words fell on my deaf ears.

"This has caused me to lose my job, Judi." His pleading was pathetic, even sadly humorous.

"Judi, I promise that our marriage will be happier than it was before."

My life with Larry flashed before my eyes. Those sarcastic words, how I had allowed everything to go his way. I saw that his every need was provided. He carried no responsibility whatsoever. He had the latest magazines on weightlifting, and all the latest equipment. His food was served when and how he wanted it. His clothes were carefully laundered along with his sex. His own car was cleaned and gassed by us. He kept to his own schedule. Everything was at our expense.

Looking at Larry I realized he couldn't believe that his paradise had come to an end. With self-loathing I saw my role and how I had silently supported him.

Larry asked me to pick up where we had left off, to work hard and keep up the facade, the characters being his slaves.

But, I was a different woman than a week ago when it all began to surface. Since then I had experienced seven days of freedom. His fairy-tale world had come to a full stop. Unknowingly I had allowed it all at the expense of my children, and I didn't know if I ever could forgive myself.

"What are you sorry for?" I asked, speaking into the phone. His dull eyes gazed at me through the glass panel between us.

"I'm sorry that I made you mad," he said.

"What made me mad?"

"I don't know but I'm sorry that you got upset with me."

"Larry, do you realize the reason that you are here in jail? I didn't file a charge against you."

"Judi," he pleaded, "you know that I didn't hurt the children. You know I love you."

"Listen to me Larry," I spoke as if to a child. "I was a witness to nothing and so did not put you here. Do you understand that? Once I reported it the Social Services picked it up and put it in the hands of the law. They are taking this thing very seriously because you abused the children. Your girls wrote reports, and your mother incriminated you. Everything you wrote and hid along with the doctor's reports did it Larry, not me."

"Judi," he insisted, as if not hearing me, "you know that you can reverse your decision and take me home, you know you can. The girls seduced me, send them away and take me back. Let me come home. I'll kill myself!"

I changed the subject, "Larry, I have to sell your collection of silver coins to help towards paying the bills. I also want you to know that I have a lawyer."

An officer tapped his shoulder to let us know our time was over.

"See you soon, Judi," he said.

"Goodbye, Larry."

I sat in silence as my brother-in-law drove me home. There was nothing to say. The girls were fussy, and wanted to know how the visit went, but didn't want to ask me directly. There was a lot of strife and conflict between us.

"He's not coming home, is he?" Debbie blurted out.

"No girls, he is not. He is going into maximum security at the state mental hospital."

None of the three of us could be happy knowing the one we had loved and trusted was now in jail. But he had kept us in jail for years. We were numb. There are no winners in a battle like this.

I went through the motions of putting the girls to bed and I laid down but couldn't sleep. Then the dam broke and tears poured out. Then I remembered the words of the prophet Jeremiah:

"My house was left unto me desolate."

And I recalled his lamentation:

"For these things I weep; mine eye, mine eye runneth down with water,

*because the comforter that should relieve
my soul is far from me: my children are
desolate, because the enemy prevailed."*

During that time there seemed to be a new surprise every day.

"Momma, Daddy told me that he had sex with several women in the church," Debbie said one day.

It really didn't shock me all that much.

"Obviously," I chided myself, "I didn't satisfy him so he went elsewhere, even taking the children. I contributed to the creation of a monster. I saw it lying there in blackness."

It hurt me to acknowledge the fact to myself because the last thing I wanted to do was to hurt my children. I was so busy keeping it all together, I couldn't see the forest for the trees. My life revolved around keeping the home together or, so I thought. What a laugh, I had been zealous but without wisdom. Larry was guilty of the sin of commission and I of the sin of omission. The girls were not to be blamed. Larry was an adult, who supposedly knew right from wrong. By setting up the situation where his every want, demand and need were met exactly to his specification, teaching our children to be subservient to him at all costs, and by placating his anger, I created the conditions which stripped them of their self-will and the God given right to say "No" to wrong.

By instilling the poison of competitiveness into the girls against me and then each other, Larry had alienated each of us into islands. They could not get along. Debbie had been especially difficult to live with. She was consumed with hurt and anger that I didn't entirely understand. Her verbal attacks on me were vitriolic. She was uncontrollably angry at times, so consumed with rage that not only her tongue lashed out at Trish and me, but she also smashed dishes and pictures — just as her dad had done.

The same pattern of hatred, frustration and abuse had transferred itself from Larry into her. It was all being played out before my eyes again through Debbie. I was weak but determined to stop it.

My attorney was a source of strength. She was a no-nonsense lawyer who knew the law and immediately went to work helping.

First, a statement of our financial condition was drawn up. I had out-earned Larry all the time we had been residents of Nebraska. Therefore, I was legally the provider of the family.

After 17 years of marriage the total value of everything we owned was only $1,800.

On August 11, she filed my first Petition for Divorce along with an affidavit of our financial condition. Only by selling our silver service, a wedding gift from Larry's parents, was I able to pay the cost of the divorce which was $1,100.

That same day we had an appointment after work with a social worker who introduced herself as Miss Dempsey. She came to the house to explain the court proceedings that were coming up. We felt comfortable with her and accepted by her.

Her personal advice came to me as a slap in the face! "Give it about six months and then have him back home for a little while."

It angered me and I thought, "Any man who rapes his children, drives his wife insane — all he can think about is satisfying his own pleasures —

tormented me for 17 years, and I prayed daily to endure, and you want me to have this man back after six months and try and make a go of it?"

My face must have revealed my thoughts for she didn't suggest this solution to me again!

I now realized that I didn't have to live in condemnation. I didn't have to be afraid for my life, or the lives of my girls. I knew that if I ever let him come back I was the one who should go into the mental hospital, not him!

Miss Dempsey said, "You're just over-reacting and taking the whole situation awfully hard!"

I couldn't help it!

I began to look back at the day the sheriff told me Larry's diagnosis — and that he was to be confined away from society — as one of the happiest days of my life.

Why?

Because I realized I wasn't the one who was sick.

But little did I realize the extent to which the court would rule my life from then on.

Every day Miss Dempsey called me. The policewoman who first called me at work the day this all began to unfold also was still involved with our case. She came to check the girls every day. Whenever I was in a crisis for the first week or two, somebody was always there. Both of these women told us that in the fall we would be required to attend special counseling classes. I mentioned this to the girls and they exploded. You would have thought that I had said we would take a walk on the moon.

"No way!" shouted Trish. "No way, Mom and that is it. Do you hear me? I ain't goin' to no counselor." Her English was terrible and her language foul.

She was purposefully obnoxious.

"You have no authority over me and can't make me go," Debbie insisted.

You can imagine my frustration.

Couldn't she see I was doing my best?

I had just been through hell with her — yet she held no respect for me or the love I had demonstrated for her.

Didn't she realize that she could be sent to a foster home under the circumstances? The counseling wasn't my idea, but that of legal authorities.

"The police and social worker said we are to have counseling." I spoke slowly and deliberately.

But down deep, I knew Debbie was right. I had no authority over her. My authority was broken so many years ago, I couldn't even remember when it was. I was her maid and caretaker. Certainly I wasn't her mother! The realization of this hit me like a deadly viper.

I called Miss Dempsey, who in turn phoned Debbie and talked to her. Under much duress she conceded she would to.

I began to struggle for my position with the children — over their father. He was no longer present, but the poisonous seeds of self-authority and rebellion certainly were. They hated him but were confused because they also loved him. All their lives he'd played with them, tucked them in at night, took them swimming and riding. I'd been separated and had unconsciously chosen to do all the chores and jobs necessary to hold the home together. I prayed and worked but, like Martha in the Bible, I was full of care and never took the time to really enjoy the children. We had not built a companionship.

What a bitter truth it was.

Letters began to arrive almost on a daily basis from Larry.

One letter said:

Dear Judi:

I am sorry that I hurt you so very, very badly. Honey, I do hope that you will not take it personally. I mean, I love you and always have since I've known you. I wasn't trying to hurt you in anyway. I really don't know what happened. I'm confused myself, but I do know I can receive the help I need and be a normal fine man again. Just please don't think I was trying in any way to hurt you. I wouldn't hurt you for anything.

I love you.

I could hardly read the letters and passed them on to my attorney. I felt guilty because Larry was in a mental hospital.

It was my failure, too. I had tried so hard to be a good wife and mother.

My emotions began playing tricks on me. I knew that he was hurting and would sob over him. The next thing I was mad at myself for what he had done to us. My emotions were like a yoyo. But I never could understand why he had little or no sense of guilt.

His letters kept coming. I found myself devouring every word, which surprised me. It was as if I had a need to be hurt over and over again. Another letter said:

Dear Judi:

I thank God that the court is heading toward rehabilitation for me as I earnestly desire that with all my heart. I will never again do what I did and I have no desire to even think of visiting home in the future unless a trained counselor says that it is okay.

I haven't found even one Christian yet, but God has forgiven me. I am His, thank God! Is anybody, anywhere praying for me?

Judi, I messed up, I failed and I am doing all in my power, everything, to get this problem corrected. They have evaluated me and decided that I do not belong in the psycho ward but have sent me to Ward 4, which specializes in treatment programs. I fully realize that all of you must really be hurt not to even write but I cannot stop writing my love for each of you.

How is your relationship with the Lord? I am so glad that when God forgives us even if we blow it, seventy times seven in one day. Didn't He tell us that if we are His that we were to forgive? This is one area in my own life that I have had trouble with.

I think of our dreams and plans of making our lives count for God. He had something wonderful for us to do. Judi, I have been doing a lot of praying and our dreams can still happen, our days ahead could be greater than anything before. I do not feel a defeat. I'm very serious, I know there could be wonderful days ahead for you and for me as a team, united in God's help and forgiveness, touching people with His love. That is the desire of my heart, to not let this failure on my part break those holy desires and secrets that we shared.

David went so far as to even deliberately murder a man but God forgave him and used him in a marvelous way.

I know that the kids are torn up now but we can talk about that, pray about that, get counseling and just go slow, miracles can happen. I am doing my part. I love you.

Please tell Trish and Debbie that their father loves them and I am proud of them. If they ever decide to write, a letter would mean so much. Remember, I am all alone here.

Well, sweet wifey, I must close soon. I do hope you are getting enough rest and taking some time for a nice little walk and to read a book and to relax. I hope you are having a nice cup of coffee every morning.

Give the kids my love.

Love, Larry

My response was terse:

Dear Larry:

The girls and I are fine. I know you want me to come and visit you but I really can't come and visit until I develop some self esteem and decide where I stand. I really don't want to see you right now. Take care of yourself.

Judi

On September 28th at 1 p.m. the girls and I had to go to a juvenile probation officer who would prepare a report to present to the court. The legal papers stated, "Not open to inspection" and were not public information. I had appeared in court before, with our foster children, the little sisters, Maggie and Frances, so I was somewhat familiar with the procedure.

But I never would have imagined what was about to happen to us.

I listened carefully to all the reports. Terms of our situation were then read aloud and concluded with the court papers which were signed by the Judge.

I made a list of the terms. Later at home the girls and I went over it.

First, we couldn't move.

Second, the girls' school progress would be closely monitored and we were expected to cooperate fully with the court. The probation officer could see the girls at anytime. We would attend two counseling programs, first one on pregnancy and how to take defensive measures, for two hours a week.

Next, I had to take a course in a parenting program, which dealt in principles of natural and logical consequence. The three of us would attend "Parents United" until next July, 10 months later. Finally, Larry was not allowed any contact with us unless permitted by the court.

It wasn't long before Debbie started in on me again.

"If you had been a good mother this would never have happened." She looked at Trish while she was speaking, refusing to face me.

"It's not her fault," Trish shouted back. "She couldn't help things ending up this way."

"I don't feel she was ever my mother at all," Debbie continued, nursing her hatred of me.

Trish stuck up for me, "Well, she tried, give her a break — eh? Daddy *was* arrested."

"That doesn't matter," Debbie shouted back. "If she had been a good mother he would never have hurt me. If she had been any kind of a mother, she would never have let him do that to me."

I stood condemned, knowing she spoke the truth.

Debbie continued to revile and curse me saying that I was the worst mother in the world. She hated me and blamed me for her shame. I was stunned time and time again, and I imagined it was something like what an animal feels being led to the slaughter.

There comes a point when you can't cope or come to terms with yourself. Getting rid of the children would have been a relief. If I hadn't been taught the Bible standard, I would have given mine away — at least temporarily.

But, I knew that God required me to be a mother to them — and to instill any mother love into them. Once the girls actually begged me to put them both in foster homes. I refused. Even though it has been painful, and my heart was broken repeatedly, I'm glad that I didn't give up on my responsibility as a mother. Today my children can't look back and say, "My mother gave me away for a while because she couldn't cope."

COUNSELING

Routines and responsibilities can contribute to healing. I tacked a new and busy schedule into place on the bulletin board in our breakfast nook.

Since the court hearing, the girls and I decided to move into a smaller apartment, using a second unlisted phone number. We were afraid that Larry might escape and find us. I was working two jobs and babysitting for friends on free evenings. We tried to get by, but barely had enough money.

Building a new life out of the chaos was not easy.

First we found that the young minister at the church we had attended, was nervous and embarrassed by our sensitive situation. There was a wall between us.

The three of us were extremely vulnerable and sensitive at this time.

Jesus Himself was fighting for a place in our lives. The other church — the one where I had sought and received help — came to mind and I introduced the girls to the pastor who had been my friend.

Church members there were the epitome of kindness.

They accepted us.

We also poured ourselves into Scouts and choir and Sunday school. The hymns and words of Jesus took on a greater depth of clarity and certainly added ointment to our bleeding souls.

We'd been anger's pawn for years, but it was hard to face the fact that some of Larry's traits, both good and bad, had rubbed off on us.

One day after school Debbie dropped her purse and school books on the floor. Out of the corner of my eye I saw a hunting knife slide out of her little red purse. Bending over I picked it up.

"Debbie, what on earth?" I questioned.

"OK, so now you know," she said. "Look Mom, what will I do if he ever comes after me? What protection do I have?"

I took the knife and realized once again something of the extensive damage Larry had dealt us all. Both girls were scared and frightened by the thought of his ever coming back. Meanwhile, my lawyer obtained several restraining orders to keep Larry from ever coming near us again.

We were under court orders to attend a "Life Adjustment Seminar" one hour each week. The girls had their own counselor who would meet with them the first hour and then with the three of us together for part of the second hour. The court had also ordered that we attend "Parents United" seminars on a weekly basis. With school, work, church and this, we were busy, but we needed to be.

Little did I realize all that the court system was going to require of me. If we had moved anywhere else other than our county in Nebraska, this could have been such a mess. The Nebraska court had recently initiated a new system for child-related sex abusers, and a new form of rehabilitation counseling.

I could see that it was my Heavenly Father who moved us right to this very spot. Only He knew where we needed to be and He put us there. He knew the resources and personnel that were available. I'm so grateful that when the ugly truth was exposed caring, responsible professionals were right there to help. I didn't have to pay a penny for all of the services that the county court system expended on our behalf. God was with us and was working as He had promised.

However as the days went by, the load became so heavy I thought I would die. My world had crumbled, I was scared, ashamed and angry. I was scared because I didn't know how to handle the new pressures associated with opening up to professional help. I had lived 17 years a married woman and never shared my inner thoughts with my husband.

When I attended "Parents United" for the first time, a social worker and coordinator led the session and a court official was present. There were five couples and myself. First names were exchanged with one another in the informal atmosphere. We took turns explaining why we were present. I found it painfully difficult to sit in the same room with men who had raped their children. Their wives sat by listening to their gruesome tales of incest.

The men spoke — in my judgment — with no sense of remorse or sorrow. They told experiences of being jailed, counseling sessions and then finally how they were allowed to return home.

I was traumatized. When I answered their questions to Larry's whereabouts, I explained that he was in the state mental hospital.

Some women in the group asked, "Why are you not planning to have your husband return home? Why are you divorcing him?"

I was intimidated, my tears uncontrollable. My heart was broken beyond repair and, what I learned seemed to increase my sense of insecurity and helplessness. My illusion of marriage and home had been destroyed and the sense of shame was beyond description. The collective heartbreak in our discussion circles each Tuesday evening was overwhelming.

As I look back from a distance of years I see the wisdom in the court's decision to submit me and the girls to this educational process. Eventually, out of it came strength and support that must be experienced to be understood. Tears still flow but less and less frequently.

My heart is mending.

Help of the sexually abused and their families is what "Parents United" was all about. That first evening I came home with some good information in my hand:

> Welcome To Parents United
> Some things to remember:
> You only need to use your first name.

Group participation is encouraged but not unless you feel comfortable about joining our discussions. If you would rather talk to someone individually, either in person or by telephone, that is OK, too. At times you may need to do both.

Remember that we cannot give a "sure cure" for any problem. Everyone is unique and will need to find their own solutions, according to what is right for them.

With this information I also reread the *Parents United Creed* which states:

* *To extend the hand of friendship, understanding, and compassion; not to judge or condemn.*
* *To better our understanding of our-selves and our children through the aid of the other members and professional guid-ance.*
* *To reconstruct and channel our anger and frustrations in other directions, not at or on our children.*
* *To realize that we are human and do have angers and frustrations; they are normal.*
* *To recognize that we do need help; we are all in the same boat; we have all been there many times.*
* *To remember that there is no miracle answer or rapid change; it has taken us years to get this way.*

> • *To have patience with ourselves, again and again and again, taking each day as it comes.*
> • *To start each day with a feeling of pro - mise, for we take only one day at a time.*
> • *To remember again that we are human; we will backslide at times.*
> • *To remember that there is always someone willing to listen and help.*
> • *To become the loving, constructive and giving parents or person that we wish to be.*

The first thing I learned was that child molesting is a curable, sick compulsion, not caused by a need for sex, but for self-destruction. The pain of hurting or destroying someone you love is far more intense and greater than just inverted destruction.

The reason is to destroy any love, warmth, or understanding that anyone may feel for you, there-fore denying that there is any within yourself.

I learned some things at "Parents United."

An explanation of the denial of incest, I was taught, is that denial is a defensive maneuver by patriarchal authority figures to protect their own power base. Patriarchy and autonomy are mutually exclusive.

Healing, I learned, is a process that takes time and cannot be rushed. To be honest, I found it hard to sit in a room full of men, knowing that they had abused their children the way my husband had done. They did not look perverted, and it would have been a lot easier to cope if they were the twisted and scarred deviants one thinks of. But they were just normal-looking men. It unnerved me. I sat beside women who had decided to stand by their men despite physical and psychological abuse to themselves and their children. They told stories of infidelity, dishonesty, bankruptcy and illness. They were women like me.

Our sessions were often depressing. Many of the fathers talked freely and nonchalantly about what they had done. There seemed to be very little in the way of repentance. After I told my story, some of the people there talked as if what had happened were my fault. Why wouldn't I let Larry come home? What was wrong with me?

We discussed the nature of rape, and its implication in incest.

It is not just an act of violence, I learned, but is a perversion which forces another type of spiritual unity between two people. The victim is simply dragged through the baseness of lust, anger, power, hatred and fear.

Another thought that was presented, was the humanistic view of sexual relations as being inconsistent with the gross humiliation that one experiences in sexual abuse of any kind. That was proof itself that we are creatures with a spirit and soul, putting us in a unique category apart from the animal realm. When one's spirit is trespassed against, the trouble begins.

Our counselor related to each one by saying that abuse, whether you are the perpetrator, victim, wife or husband, is not a fate worse than death. But a lifetime of bitterness is. By using hatred and revenge to retaliate against wrongs done to us, we become the biggest losers. No one disagreed with her.

For me, the first step to recovery was to open up the darkness that filled my soul and willingly ask my Heavenly Father to come and heal me. The next step was to forgive Larry but it took me years to release the hold of bitterness and humiliation he had inflicted upon us.

I wish I could say it was a miraculous and instant process. It was not, but our God is a God of hope. He is bigger than our past and He is the door to our future.

I was clinging desperately to Him, to the girls, and to the professional help the court knowingly provided.

For years I had mistakenly believed that if you loved somebody, he'd have to love you back. Of course now I understood how naive I was.

A 50-year-old woman in our group described her husband as an emotional sadist who shredded her self-esteem through constant insults, put-downs, complaints and criticisms.

Love, we learned, is the difference between show and tell. Love is a behavior, not simply a word. While her husband spoke of love, all he showed was contempt. To stand by such a person indefinitely invited victimization. It's a Catch-22 situation. The person you stand by has no reason to alter his behavior. But first the woman needs a reason to alter her own masochistic pattern.

Professional counseling gave many of us wives, scared and scarred by hurtful men, the first inklings to understand and to believe that what we feel, and think, matters. It is sad that we had to be taught and made to understand that what we want, as human beings, matters. We are entitled to have rights in a relationship.

If your husband is telling you you're rotten and you believe him, something is seriously wrong. This is unacceptable behavior, I happily learned.

A great many women mistake need for love. Some hoped one would substitute for the other by using the excuse of giving, giving and giving. I had hoped that Larry's need for me could take the place of the love I knew he did not feel for me. I felt that a love for need relationship — if you love me, I will fill your needs — was the same as a love for love type of relationship. It never is, and it never can be. Many wives in my class felt they weren't meeting all their husband's needs and punished themselves through self-destructive behavior, like overeating or drinking. If you really do believe it's all your fault, you think you deserve to be fat and depressed and unlovable. You say "the hell with me, I don't deserve better." Ultimately, some women simply surrender.

Admitting that we're trapped in a nightmare is excruciatingly difficult for most women. It's not always the dumb, ugly, useless women that no one else would have, that live with men that abuse them. Yet many women stay with their abusive husbands because their partners need them so much.

A battered wife who returned again and again to her abusive husband asked plaintively, "Who would love him if I left?"

Most of my male relationships from childhood were built upon my doing things for them. I see that now and am working on caring for myself as well as for others. In therapy I learned that many wives reported discovering for the first time that self-respect is a new-found freedom. If love is meant to prevail, it will without the husband taking more than you can give.

Sounds selfish? Perhaps, but I have learned that love and honor are selfish things, especially when we need to survive.

The wives who left their husbands in order to survive actually seemed anything but selfish. All they wanted, in many cases, was the security and serenity that they never had in their marriages.

One battered wife talked about the relief of being able to "lie down and go to sleep knowing she wasn't going to be awakened by a madman in the middle of the night." That feeling was worth all the courage it took for her to walk out the door.

Would your husband stand by you if you acted exactly as he did? If the answer is no, all the love in the world can't change it to a yes. Despite their fears, the women who leave often fall apart.

This brand-new sense of deserving someone who loves rather than leans came through clearly. I learned that you cannot put a price tag on personal self-worth and, most importantly, I have learned that I just have to be me.

Therapy for children is different from that for adults. Psychologists use puppets or toys to help a child play out her feelings. The focus of the therapy is the same for all ages: to correct the basic misconception that the abuse happened because "I was bad."

This fallacy is the key to all the symptoms and problems that develop as a child grows up. Therapy means facing frightening memories and bottled-up anger. It's often harder for a victim to work through anger at the non-abusive mother than at the abusive father.

The victim also has to face the uncertainty about whether the mother did know what was happening with the father. That's more difficult to work through than anger at the father, who was definitely guilty.

If a victim can express her anger to a therapist or supportive friends or family members, the anger often plays itself out. It wouldn't stay with her daily for the rest of her life.

A child needs to know that God made her body and that it's beautiful. God gave her body to her and she doesn't have to let anyone touch it in ways that make her feel funny, afraid or bad!

Children need to be taught that it is all right to say "No" to an adult. This is the chapter that Dr. Spock left out. We teach our children to be quiet, to obey, to always be good. We teach them to be perfect victims. Instead, kids should learn that there are certain things that no adult, even a relative, has a right to ask.

Forcing your child to hug and kiss "Uncle Charlie" or others, when they don't want to, can be damaging. The message is: "My parents say I'm suppose to submit myself to things that are distasteful or uncomfortable to me." Children need to sense parental protection. Remember, almost all child abuse is done by people the children know.

Don't keep secrets where sexual abuse is concerned. Children should be encouraged to talk and parents should listen.

But there's a deeper reason children don't talk about sexual abuse. Incest is much more than the violation of a child's body. It's the ultimate betrayal of their protectors, comforters, and closest friends. While they are suffering the most severe form of emotional abuse, their loyalty and love for their abuser make it nearly impossible for them to speak up. Awkwardness, repulsion, resentment, confusion, guilt and fear create a dungeon from which there seems to be no escape.

Though innocent, they feel dirty, ashamed, and different, sensing the wrongness of the situation. Shame and fear work together to keep a stranglehold on a child's ability to call out for help.

"Don't blame yourself!" Children should be taught, even before anything happens to them. Sexual abuse is not the victim's fault.

Children should be taught to trust their instincts. If they feel uncomfortable with the hugs and kisses from a relative or friend, parents should not encourage them to put up with it just for the sake of avoiding a fuss.

The child gets the message something is wrong only when secrecy is introduced such as "Don't tell your Mommy that we did that" or "she won't love you anymore."

Another reason children don't tell is that the abuser is usually someone they trust at first, often someone they depend on for affection and approval.

Sexual exploitation is often introduced at a very young age and disguised as a game. The most common experience is genital fondling. The daughter wakes up to find her father in bed beside her. Or, he steps into the shower with her. A small child feels trapped.

Part of the agony of the child dragged through our criminal justice system as a witness to his or her own sexual abuse by a father is that, not infrequently, the father is the more nurturing parent.

With a mother who is either chronically ill or emotionally unavailable, the only nurturing the child receives may have come from the father. Youngsters want the abuse to end. But they don't want their only source of love amputated.

An abusive parent is the key figure in establishing a child's self image. It may take the better part of a lifetime to shut off the internal voice of the father who betrayed a child, the inner voice that whispers, "You are bad. And you'll be sorry if you tell."

A person betrayed in their most significant early relationships finds it hard to learn how to trust other people or to take the risks that are necessary in establishing lasting relationships.

VICTIMS

Miss Dempsey, the wise and empathetic counselor who was assigned to Debbie and Trish in August, simply was known as Carol to us. She described the girls to me as being like puppies who had been run over. Anyone who goes to pick up the injured creatures will get bitten, even though they are trying to help them.

The girls hated each other.

They were angry. They hated me. We went through some very tough days. Actually, for the next two years we struggled to maintain equilibrium just trying to cope with this disaster and each other. Condemnation tried to sink us more than once. Trish resisted change, especially in the beginning of the counseling sessions, and immediately asked to be allowed to go to a foster home.

"Good!" was Debbie's response. "We'll be rid of you. Go ahead." Trish tried to control me with anger, exactly like Larry did for years.

Pressures would build and the girls would join forces and turn on me. The torment was my taskmaster once again and inadequacy was there to point a bony finger at all of my weaknesses and faults as a parent. It was a battle that had to be fought daily with the living Word of God and faith and salvation and deliverance that is in Jesus' name.

Just before Christmas, Carol called me in for a progress report.

"Well," she sighed, "we are making progress with the girls. I know it doesn't seem like it or feel like it but we are!"

Then she continued, "The girls are in what we call the 'rage stage' now. They are expressing fury at their father for his action, anger at the culture for its ban of silence and indignation with the church for ignoring this aspect of our world's brokenness. Hatred is vented against you for not doing something sooner. They are victims of grief because of the lack of a trustworthy relationship with their dad, for the death that they experienced each time he abused them. There is also anguish in hating their father."

She looked up from the report to see if I was still with her and drew a deep breath before going on.

"They internalized this abuse for long years, and it's actually healthier to express their agony which they are doing now. It's a dark triangle that is being released through their emotional remembrance, as painful as it is. This release is the key to their recovery, and they must express it all along the pathway to healing. They are fighting the knowledge that because of the abuse they are different, isolated and alone. As a result, your daughters are fearful, angry and mistrusting, and easily intimidated by males. They have been alienated from half of God's creation. They have the need to control. It's not conscious, but is retained in their behavior. This is why they make fun of church and all it represents. God is portrayed as male. He is a Father that they cannot relate to at this time.

"They find it hard to believe that anyone, including God, could really love them. Guilt riddles their self-assurance. The key to their healing is compassion — ours, and God's. Because their natural father was not sure of his own masculinity, and carried a huge deprivation in the depths of his being for unconditional love and acceptance, he grabbed at love but in the wrong way. In so doing he opened a gulf between the girls and himself and the essence of life itself. This has had a devastating effect upon all that they were taught or thought about God. They see their natural father as a type of the Heavenly One, hence the confusion. They are groping and do want a way out of the severe damage that has crippled them. They act tough to give them a protective coat. It will take time for them to be free, to be truly soft and feminine again in their thinking, which at present seems like a weakness synonymous with vulnerability."

Then she added, "Intellectually your girls are leaps ahead of most boys their ages, but emotionally the scars keep them bound to the past and its ugly flashbacks of scared little girls at the mercy of a 6-foot, 5-inch molester. They wonder, 'Will all men be like my father, showing me off in the daylight and groping at me and hurting me in the night?' "

Carol stopped. She could see that I was having a hard time understanding what she was saying. The hurt was still part of every breath I breathed, as constant and predictable as my next pulse beat.

"Carol, I am grateful that you've been able to spend this kind of time with my girls," I said. "It's just so hard for me to bear it all."

I broke down and cried. She understood and let me cry it all out. A deep longing — intense in its yearning — filled my heart.

"Oh, to get into life, into the sunshine, into a little love, just a little love," I told Carol. "There has to be a stopping off place for this pain. Sometime, somewhere it will no longer be there to meet us every moment."

"You will all come through," Carol advised. "It takes time to heal."

Then she asked me, "Would you like to read a little from the girl's files? Debbie has gone into some detail of the actual abuse she suffered referred to as sexual atrocities by the court.

"I have terrifying memories," the counselor read from Debbie's file:

> "I never felt secure or safe ... I was drowning and never had strength to call for help. Like a corpse, I lay there wishing I were dead. I was a trapped animal. Not only was I desperate then, I still am and the hate only grows. He slowly and decidedly destroyed me and I hate him. I already felt dirty because of my father's abuse and to top if off, he called me ugly names making me

feel like it was all my fault! I felt like there was something terribly wrong with me that the other kids didn't have wrong with them. I knew this didn't happen to every-one. I wondered what made me different. I thought there must be something I did to cause my dad to do this. A dark cloud seemed to hang over my head all the time."

Sensing my pain, Carol paused briefly, then continued reading, "I never would have initiated those encounters on my own. It was my dad's idea — not mine!"

"What about Trish? Is she as damaged as Debbie?"

My voice was almost inaudible.

Carol had established a rapport with each of us and we felt she was a friend, and never once did any of us sense the slightest condemnation or judgmental attitude. It would have put us over the edge for sure. Shame just tainted everything. Shame that separates and then snares. If the truth were to be known, the real battle goes on in a person's spirit. There is a war for control. The knowledge of the Bible and healing scriptures were the only force I personally found that could dislodge such other forces as shame, self-hate and condemnation.

Trish's file was opened.

"She is a completely different child, reacting in ways, opposite to Debbie," Carol explained.

I knew that just living with the girls.

"Unfortunately Trish keeps most of the abuse locked deep inside. It is going to take more time to help free her," Carol said.

Carol read from the file:

"I love my family very much, but I can't separate them from the scary memories. I keep asking why didn't anyone help me, why did this happen? I never slept well at night because I never knew when Dad would tiptoe down the stairs, and open my door. He was like a kid playing a game, but he was too big and I couldn't win. I guess mostly I remember how he told me about Debbie and how good she was ... I felt like screaming. It was like I was being stabbed and it hurt me for days after. It hurt when I walked and when I sat in school, and it was all I could ever think of, so ugly and so mean. I knew I was a failure, because I felt I was."

8

DID YOU KNOW?

During the months of counseling, I took down notebooks of facts, statistics, and case histories because everything was bringing some degree of understanding to our lives.

One of the first things I was taught is that there is no stereotypical incest offender, although in therapy certain patterns of behavior and similar family histories begin to emerge. For example, incest and alcoholism seem to go hand in hand.

At work, I was surprised by my boss's reaction to our situation. He would not concede that educated, professional people encountered this unspeakable curse. I disagreed with him and mentioned some of the professions represented in my counseling session.

He just turned a deaf ear to me and said, "Bring me statistics of a socio-economic breakdown of the number of incidents in relation to the professions and the Judeo-Christian ethic."

Where would I get proof like that? I wondered. In just the last 10 years, the cry of victims of incest has begun to be heard in America and around the world. Incest has been kept under a blanket of shame and secrecy and is one of our most under-reported crimes. This conspiracy of silence has served to protect the offender, concealing his victim. For generations victims have felt betrayed, shamed and rejected. Therefore, they kept silent and remained victims. The true message should be, "Don't hide it, you are not alone, and you can be helped."

Many victims did not know or fully realize how much they hurt, how much pain they had absorbed until it became okay to recognize it. We mothers feel our own pain and deal with it at the same time. We must be supportive of our children who have so little going for them in a situation of incest.

Inadequate bonding with one's parents and lack of early physical contact and involvement with one's child were the two best predictors of sexual abuse. The incestuous fathers were more likely than the others to report that they had been neglected or mistreated by their parents. As parents they had spent minimal time in the home during the child's first three years and had little involvement in nurturing and caring for their daughters.

Between 15 and 34 percent of all girls, and three and nine percent of all boys are victims of sexual abuse each year, according to the Family Violence Research Program at the University of New

Hampshire. Father-daughter sexual abuse accounts for about 25 percent of incest cases; stepfather-stepdaughter for another 25 percent; and abuse by brothers, uncles, grandfathers, brothers in-law and cousins account for the remaining 50 percent.[1]

Most children keep their traumas a tightly held secret. Other victims develop immediate symptoms: not sleeping or eating, temper tantrums or bed wetting. Others who mask their anxieties for years create what experts call a "psycological time bomb." Guilt, confusion, depression and passivity can suddenly explode into such self-destructive behavior as promiscuity, alcohol, drug abuse and even suicide. Long-term symptoms include detachment from others, and frightening flashbacks.

The average period of abuse is seven years.

Incest is strictly avoided in most human cultures. Yet, it is estimated that every year as many as 250,000 children in the U.S. are sexually molested in their homes, with 75 percent of these incidents taking place between fathers and daughters.[2]

"Over the last two years, the abuse rate in America has grown approximately 80 percent. The average sexually abused child is between the ages of ten and eleven years of age. The earliest abuse is between the ages of three and four and extends up the age of eighteen. In sexual abuse there are four times as many girls abused as boys. All the statistics reflect parental role in the abuse," according to a

---

[1] Child Assault Prevention Project, Columbus, Ohio

[2] "The Unspeakable Family Secret," *Psychology Today*, May, 1984

group called Little Ones, Inc., P.O. Box 3006, San Luis Obispo, California, 93403.

Lack of disclosure is a discouraging factor that helps keep sexual exploitation patterns moving from one generation to the next.

Genital fondling was the activity most common in childhood.

Attempted rape, unwanted vaginal intercourse, and genital fondling were the activities reported as stressful, unwanted experiences in adolescence.

One national magazine reported that 75 percent of the adolescent prostitutes interviewed in a Minneapolis study had been victims of incest. The same article reports a high percentage of adolescent drug addicts as having been caught in some form of family sexual abuse, and names sexual abuse as a significant factor in adolescent runaways."

Mother plays a role of perpetuating the incest, as did the father, even though legally she was innocent. Most studies suggest that while the mother may not allow the fact of the incest into her conscious awareness, she is most often aware of it.

It may be quite open, and the mother bluntly says to her daughter, "Tonight it is your turn to sleep with your father."

Sometimes it is more subtle, as the mother who leaves the daughter sitting on the father's lap when she goes out and calls back for her to take good care of Daddy.

One factor upon which most researchers agree is that incest rarely begins with rape or actual intercourse.

Robert Geiser reports, "There is usually a progression of sexual contact over a considerable period of time. Most commonly it begins with

exhibitionism. This leads eventually to mastur-
bation, and other fondling.[3] This statistic lines up
perfectly with Debbie and Trish's experience.

There is a great difference in the duration of
incestuous "affairs." The average lasts somewhere
between two and three years. A very few are one-
time-only contacts. Some continue for more than
eight years.

America is not alone in this struggle to combat
sexual abuse. The following statistics from Canada
got our attention, too:

> "The problem of child sexual abuse in
> Canada is so pervasive and deep rooted that
> in its response to our recommendations,
> we believe that the Government of Canada
> must establish a means to deal adequately
> and on a coordinated basis with these issues
> to provide protection for sexually abused
> and exploited children and youths. This
> strongly held concern is national in scope.
> It cuts across all social, religious and poli-
> tical boundaries. It encompasses all forms
> of sexual abuse of the child, whether this
> involves sexual assault, juvenile prosti-
> tution or the making of child pornography.
> "At sometime during their lives, about
> one in two females and one in three males
> have been victims of one or more un-
> wanted sexual acts. These acts include:
> being exposed to; being sexually threatened;
> being touched on a sexual part of the body;

---

[3] Geiser, "Hidden Victims," pg. 13

and attempts of assault or being sexually assaulted," according to the 1984 Sexual Offenses Against Children in Canada Summary of the report of the Committee on Sexual Offences Against Children and Youths appointed by the Ministry of Justice and Attorney General of Canada and the Ministry of National Health and Welfare.

9

MOLESTERS OR FATHERS?

I have learned a little about what causes certain men to become child abusers.

By definition, I learned that a pedophile is a person who is sexually attracted to children. Child molesters are not insane and they are not sexually frustrated, according to "A Study of the Child Molester Myths and Realities," an article published in the Journal of the American Criminal Justice System.

Most abusers are not dirty old men. Many appear to be quite respectable.

Most are relatively young. In one study, only 10 percent of the assailants were found to be older than 50.

Also most child molesters are well known to their victims, and abusers were abused themselves as children.

Our counselors taught us about the nature of lust. Lust cannot be equated with the normal sex drive. It gnaws at the afflicted person with no amount of gratification bringing relief. Every experience is found wanting, physically and emotionally, leaving its victim looking for yet another means of some gratification.

The sexual offender may be passive and inhibited or active and assertive, gentle or violent, religious or irreligious, masculine or effeminate. He may hate his mother, love his mother, or be ambivalent about her. He may have had a repressive sexual development or he may have been overstimulated. And we could go on with these polar opposites.

But what there is in common is a serious defect in interpersonal relationships. There is an absence of mature, selfless concern for the victim of his obsession, an inability to love in a desexualized manner, a terrible sadness and sense of loneliness, a lack of sublimation, and a totally narcissistic, self-centered orientation.

In general the experts say that child molesters tend to be weak, insecure men who need to feel that they are loved and are in control of a relationship.

Some researchers divide molesters into two general categories:

• The **fixated offender** often claims to be in love with the children and is a pedophile with a history of years of molesting. Frequently abused themselves as youngsters, these people are loners who become fixated on prepubescent children, often conforming their sexual appetite to just girls or just boys. Many of them wallow in self pity.

• In contrast **regressed molesters** may have led normal married lives for years. Their sexual involvement with children may be triggered by sudden stress, such as a midlife crisis.

"An example would be an adult male of about 40, his marriage dissolves and he gets involved with a step-daughter," says Dr. Michael Cos, director of the Sex Offender Treatment Program at the Baylor College of Medicine in Houston, Texas.

Other research shows that the victims of sadistic sexual abuse cope with repeated assaults by developing multiple personalities, a dozen or so on the average and sometimes more than 100 separate identities.

"I became another little girl so he couldn't hurt me," one child told New York social worker Flora Colao.

The pedophile's experiences with his girls are, in his mind, romantic experiences and he may truly believe he is in love with them. His level of understanding of life and love is very childlike. He lives in a fantasy world and still tries to believe Cinderella lived happily ever after. He has experienced the realities of life, found them distasteful and tries to return to his Cinderella world. He is generally very polite, kind and appears to be genuinely concerned — which preys on a child's vulnerability.

He is a somewhat successful man, at least to the limits of his education and abilities. He may have been rejected by a wife or adult girlfriend but otherwise is accepted by society and is probably a respected citizen of the community.

Society has not rejected him; he has rejected society.

The child molester has troubles with society as a whole. He has generally been rejected by society or thinks he has and is unstable in his work habits, unable to function socially and is a loner. He has nowhere to escape but to the child's world. Sex becomes his escape mechanism.

As much as parents do not wish to admit it, they must realize their lives are the examples that their children will follow. If the mother is of immoral character and allows her boyfriend to move in then it is certain the eight year old will have her own boyfriend. Chances are it will be a man.

First, the child is looking for a replacement for her daddy.

Second, she feels further rejection because some other man is stealing attention from the mom that she feels is hers.

Many single parents, and married ones also, are so wrapped up in self that they actually pawn their children off on a molester, to get the "brats" out of their hair.

This rejection of the child plays right into the hands of the molester.

Most child molesters were exploited and victimized when they were young children. So they learn from an early age how to be victimized and how to victimize others. They start victimizing others, not necessarily in sexual ways, very early.

The molester is a five or six or seven-year-old child in a grown man's body. He's scared. He decided 30 years ago that he wouldn't ever deal with this issue. He has trained himself and rehearsed himself for 25 to 30 years not to reveal this secret. Yet all the time he's longed for someone to be close to him. You can't pull the real person out of him. He is like someone drowning.

Child abuse is rarely an isolated incident and, unless legal pressure is brought to bear, the abuse may go on for years abusing generations of children.

If the taboo is ever broken, it may become easy for a parent to find reasons to justify continuing sexual activity.

Fathers in our counseling sessions made comments as follows:

> *"It shows how much I love the child. How precious she is to me."*
> *"It brings us closer together."*
> *"It's a wonderful kind of sex education."*
> *"It's the only really tender, pure kind of sex I can enjoy. I deserve some outlet."*
> *"It doesn't really hurt anyone."*
> *"Its that feeling of wanting and being close to them, of wanting to control them. Little people are easier to control than big people."*
> *"I know I was doing wrong. But I didn't feel it."*
> *"I thought, 'There's nobody better than me.'*
> *"I did what I wanted to. The sun rose and set on me."*
> *"I thought about the children but not enough to stop doing it."*
> *"I liked the feeling of control and the love I felt towards the children."*
> *"You tell yourself that they want it."*

> *"I felt a lot of loneliness. My wife neglected me a lot."*
> *"I blamed mine on alcohol and stress."*
> *"I was depressed. I was angry. I guess I could say I was looking for revenge or something."*
> *"I used force and anger to get my way."*
> *"I would take something and throw it up against the wall so they would freeze."*

In the counseling sessions each one of us was given opportunity to learn from one another's mistakes as we delved into our various backgrounds, sharing some of the attitudes stated above.

"Which child molesters are treatable?" asked our counselors.

None of us had an answer.

"The key thing is how much is the molester admitting to his responsibility for the crime," she said.

This, we learned, is where confession and repentance are vital keys. Some molesters have been feeling a general guilt all along. Some just a little; others feel none and never will.

Once caught, child molesters are slow to accept the fact that they did anything wrong. They offer lots of excuses. They blame their behavior on alcohol, or the wife.

Some common excuses include:

> *"It's her fault."*
> *"People don't understand me."*

"You're acting like the child didn't like it and I know she did."
"I didn't really hurt her."
"Nobody knows the loneliness I've suffered."[1]

These people are good at manipulation. They're among the best in the world.

Their survival in their crime hinges on their ability to cover it up. Their guilt cannot be hidden behind drugs, alcohol, or lies, and it cannot be erased.

There must be an acknowledging, confessing and turning from it forever, one day at a time.

Molesters do hurt children, sometimes physically and almost always in spirit. The bodily damage can include torn vaginas and rectums and veneral disease or pregnancy. More excessive sexual abuse leads to more extensive damage.

Victims suffer from nightmares, hyperalertness, insomnia and flashbacks. These same symptoms of post-traumatic stress disorder were found in combat victims returned from Vietnam. The child is constantly on guard, yet is trapped and feels helpless.

Power struggles, blackmail, jealously, guilt and fear prevent normal personal or sexual development for the child involved. She or he finds severe

---

[1] Tim Hodges, a consultant at Henrico County Mental Health Center and coordinator of sex offense treatment programs for the State Department of Corrections.

problems trying to relate to appropriate sexual partners later on.[2]

Everyone suffers and the suffering is intensified by the repulsion and rejection of all the "decent" people who are afraid to recognize the problem and take appropriate measures to deal with it.

Even when molesters are convicted, judges are reluctant to send them to prison. Behind bars, sex offenders are likely to be beaten, raped or even murdered by other convicts, who despise "diddlers." Most prisons offer no therapy for child molesters. Accordingly, judges often sentence offenders to probation, requiring them to get therapy. The molester knows that if he sings the right song and dances the right dance, he'll be out a lot quicker.

The most striking similarities among incestuous families were the fathers' tendency to tyrannize and the mother's fear of questioning his absolute authority. The tyranny may be a facade. People always think of the father as an aggressive autocrat, but in many cases, he's like a child."[3]

According to "Child Pornography and Sex Rings," an article published by the Federal Bureau of Investigation, pedophiles often collect children.

They take pictures of the children they molest and keep a collection of kiddieporn. Pedophile underground membership societies and pornographic literature exist nationwide, according to

---

[2] Jay Howell, Executive-Director of the Justice Department's new National Center for Missing and Exploited Children.

[3] Hank Giarretto of San Jose, California, Director of Parents United which helps adults, victims and offenders alike to cope with the consequences of child molestation.

Seth L. Goldstein, Inspector in the office of the District Attorney in San Jose, California.

We also learned that abusers can be helped.

Abusers and their children are both victims caught in a vicious cycle. It is important to note that:

> • *Most abusive parents love their children very much, but not very well.*
> • *The majority of abusers were abused themselves as children;*
> • *For most abusers, treatment and rehabilitation can produce positive results.*
> • *It is vitally important that a means for the abuser to get help is provided. Reporting child abuse or suspected child abuse becomes the first step in this helping process.*

The Bible sets the highest but not impossible standard for human relationships and if we live by the rules we can expect the promised blessings. If not, we suffer from nothing less than a curse:

> *"He who conceals his transgression will not prosper, but he who confesses and forsakes them will find compassion,"* Proverbs 28:13.
> *"Let the wicked forsake his way, and the unrighteous man his thoughts; and let him return to the Lord, and He will have compassion on him. He will abundantly pardon,"* Isaiah 55:7.

FATHERHOOD

What is the standard set for a father? Our lives were so twisted that this question hardly seemed important, yet it kept working it's way back into my thinking during those trying days.

Many years later I received satisfying answers other than what I had learned in counseling classes, when I had the priviledge of hearing Dr. Derek Prince teach on the subject of Fatherhood.

The fatherhood of God is eternal. I learned the position of fatherhood in the here and now is God's earthly projection of sanctity and importance in human experience and time. I pictured God as having a heavenly family after discovering the word "house" in John, chapter 14 is synonymous with "family." Family life has its origin in eternity, in the relationship between the Godhead. I began to think of God as my daddy or father and Heaven as my personal home, and place of belonging. It helped the Scriptures to come alive and into focus:

> "For this cause I bow my knees unto the Father of our Lord Jesus Christ, of whom the whole family in Heaven and earth is named," Ephesians 4:14, 15.

Jesus promised us,

> "In my Father's house are many man-sions ..." (families), John 14:2.

I learned from Dr. Prince that because God the Father is head of Christ, the marriage relationship is a projection of an eternal relationship. This gives us the godly pattern of authority. I had always responded to authority; but as a slave with no rights rather than an equal. According to the Bible, my place was one of inferiority. There was my big mistake. Eve was Adam's co-inheritor and co-equal. God's Word says it like this:

> "But I would have you know, that the head of every man is Christ, and the head of the woman is the man; and head of Christ is God," I Cor. 11:3.

Jesus is the perfect example of what one's relationship with his father should be. He said,

> "I and my father are one," John 10:30.

Here are two more verses which give us insight:

> "Ye have heard how I said unto you, I go away, and come again unto you. If ye loved me, ye would rejoice because I said, I go unto the Father; for my Father is greater than I," John 14:28.

> "Let this mind be in you which was also in Christ Jesus," Phil. 2:5.

Jesus lives in obedience to his Father. Though being subject, he was also one with the Father. So is the wife with her husband. I knew nothing of this kind of relationship in our marriage and it seemed almost too idealistic for me to grasp as possible in real life.

I read how the Father honors and exalts the Son and the Son honors and exalts the Father. And we have the exciting promise of God being everything at the end of the ages:

> *"And when all things shall be subdued unto him, then shall the Son also himself be subject unto him that put all things under him, that God may be all in all,"* I Cor. 15:28.

This lofty example is to be implemented in everyday marriages. The husband is to honor and esteem and respect his wife. In fact, he is to love his wife as himself!

Well, in my case, Larry hated himself, so how could he ever have loved me or the girls?

The Heavenly Father will not receive any slight against His Son, and husbands are to do likewise, and in this way the stigma of inferiority will be broken.

Inferiority was written upon all of us. But, according to the Bible, this honoring and giving honor and respect in marriage is a direct projection into time of the relationship of the Godhead. Our homes on earth are to be reproductions of the home above prepared by our Father where Father-hood, headship and fellowship exist in perfect balance and love.

In the Gospels, Jesus prays that we may have perfect unbroken fellowship here because this is the pattern of Heaven:

> *"That they all may be one; as thou, Father, art in me, and I in thee, that they also may be one in us: that the world may believe that thou hast sent me. And the glory which thou gavest me, I have given them: that they may be one, as we are one,"* John 17: 21, 22.

God's Word was designed to be the theme song of the home. Growing up a minister's daughter, I of course knew and had experienced this. I was surprised to learn that in every dispensation represented in the Bible, the place and importance of the home took preeminence as seen by the following promises:

> *"Therefore shall ye lay up these words in your heart and in your soul, and bind them for a sign upon your hand, that they may be as frontlets between your eyes.*
> *"And ye shall teach them to your children, speaking of them when thou sittest in thine house, and when thou walkest by the way, when thou liest down and when thou risest up.*
> *"And thou shalt write them upon the door posts of thine house, and upon thy gates: That your days may be multiplied, and the days of your children, in the land which the Lord sware unto your fathers to*

give them, as the days of Heaven upon the earth," Deut. 11:18-21.

Family life here is referred to "as the days of heaven upon the earth." Knowledge that this promise was in the Bible took my breath away. It was almost too good to be true. Yet, I had read volumes of books about happy marriages and homes, longing to see into a marriage of love.

The home also must be our shelter, our protective abode, where children are nourished up in quietness and confidence receiving and reciprocating the love and respect of parents, of God and one another.

The average child forms his basic concepts of God from his natural father. No father can ever delegate this spiritual responsibility to another, not even his wife. It is his, and his alone.

A renegade reneges from his primary responsibilities as husband, father and spiritual leader in the home.

Every father has two specific ministries: as the priest he represents his family to God, and as a prophet he represents God to his family.

Larry was a minister who never ministered to his own. I see it even more clearly now and don't hate him for it, I just ache because of the empty, hurtful, lost years.

God's primary qualification for spiritual leadership is in relation to how the father cares for his family. This may come as a shock to ministry-oriented individuals. The Bible gives stunning examples of men who were chosen by God because they were good fathers:

"Come thou and all thy house into the ark for thee have I seen righteous in this generation," Gen. 7:1.

Noah, his wife and sons and daughters in law were saved because of Noah's relationship to the Lord.

Of Abraham, the Lord says:

"For I know him that he will command his children and his household after him and they shall keep the way of the Lord, to do justice and judgment," Gen. 18:19.

God was obligated to honor Joshua who boldly stated:

"As for me and my house we will serve the Lord," Joshua 24:15.

Job was a very concerned and loving father. We read that he offered sacrifice every week for his children:

"Job sent and sanctified them, and rose up early in the morning, and offered burnt offerings according to the number of them all: for Job said, It may be that my sons have sinned and cursed God in their hearts. Thus did Job continually," Job 1:5.

Fathers are warned not to overtax their children. A father's relationship with the Lord will be reflected in his interactions with those under his own roof:

> *"Ye fathers, provoke not your children to wrath, bring them up in the nurture, (education) of the Lord,"* Eph. 6:4.

Paul spoke life and hope to the Roman jailer by saying:

> *"Believe on the Lord Jesus Christ and thou shalt be saved and thy house,"* Acts 16:31.

It is a staggering fact that the husband and father is given the power of choice to decide the destiny of whole families, for good or for evil. We read the story of the distraught father bringing his epileptic son to Jesus and crying:

> *"... If thou canst do anything, have compassion on us and help us,"* Mark 9:22.

But Jesus put the primary responsibility back upon the father and said,

> *"If thou canst believe, all things are possible to him that believeth,"* Mark 9:23.

When fathers fail to live in an obedient relationship with the Lord, a curse results.
"What is the curse?" you may ask.
Our sophisticated thought processes say, "We don't have curses today. That is something out of the dark ages."

The curse is wrong family life, evidenced by broken homes. It is the father's responsibility to turn to God first, not the families. He is held accountable for setting the standard in the home and he will one day give account for the innocent lives that were wasted and destroyed which were under his authority. Whether a father happens to believe this has nothing to do with the fact that he still remains responsible. Because of runaway fathers, today we don't have to look past most front doors to see the results of the curse, as prophesied in the Word of God:

> "... if thou wilt not hearken unto the voice of the Lord thy God, thou shalt beget sons and daughters, but thou shalt not enjoy them," Deut. 28:15, 41.

Why is this happening? Simply because fathers are not fulfilling their responsibilities as set down by the eternal Word of God:

> "My people are destroyed for lack of knowledge; because thou hast rejected knowledge, I will also reject thee, that thou shalt be no priest to me: seeing thou hast forgotten the law of thy God, I will also forget thy children," Hosea 5:6.

But, there is hope for the father who confesses his sin and repents and receives forgiveness for his filthy deeds which only a Holy God can abolish by the blood sacrifice of His Son Jesus Christ:

"... *unto them that turn from transgression in Jacob, this is my covenant with them, saith the Lord: My Spirit that is upon thee, and my words which I have put in thy mouth, shall not depart out of thy mouth, nor out of the mouth of thy seed, nor out of the mouth of thy seed's seed saith the Lord, from henceforth and forever,"* Isaiah 59:20, 21.

The Bible affirms that the words of life must first be in the father's mouth and stay there and then they will reside and also live in the lives of his offspring down to his great grandchildren.

This study crystalized my understanding of the absolute authority of God's Word and plan for mankind. In our own personal lives, Larry and I were reaping the bitter fruit of his broken relationship with the Lord first, then with each other, and lastly with our girls.

You may scoff at the word "curse" but the girls and I are living examples of brokenness. Our lives are proof of what happens when a father flaunts and ignores the Word of a holy and righteous God.

10

LETTERS

Larry continued to write from the state hospital:

Dear Judi:

I realize that I have failed terribly, yet I must make it clear that I have never stopped loving you. If you could see me as a man with an emotional problem, which is solvable, and who still loves you with all his heart and who never in anyway wanted to hurt you, it would be so much better.

I went to call you this morning and I discovered you had changed the number. I am not angry just hurt, that I cannot even talk to the precious ones who have been the center of my life since 1964.

Judi, I hope that you will not let anger and bitterness utterly consume you. I admit

I have failed, and failed badly. Must I be destroyed because I have failed? I am isolated here with no encouragement at all. You know when you really get down to it there is really not much incentive for me to try. Can you not at least try to forgive?

I feel this situation is not hopeless. You can forgive you know, I mean from the heart and with God's love and power and excellent counseling from the Social Services I feel that we could definitely heal our family and it would be far stronger than ever before.

To just shut me out completely is almost more than I can bear. You at least can get outside, go to the store, walk in the sun, and you have a home and family to fight for. I have nothing and despite my best efforts my resolve to try is weakening daily.

I do not ask for pity and if you really cannot find it in your heart to forgive and get back together as a happy-normal-well-adjusted family, then forget me. I do feel in the long run you will regret it for not at least trying. I want to make it clear, I have no desire at all for divorce, I love you with all my heart. This marriage does not have to end in divorce, it can be one of the strongest, happiest and fulfilling marriages of all time if we would but allow it to. I am willing, are you?

Will you please let me love you with a depth that you have never known? I will devote my life to you and be your husband in the truest sense of the word and your lover. You may have fears such as Debbie saying if I come back she would leave home. Honey, with a marriage counselor and professional help, we could go very slowly and discuss this and I definitely feel this could be worked out.

What happened in our home will never happen again. In a few short years the kids will be gone and we could have a wonderful, happy, romantic life together, far more fun and rewarding than we can imagine. A counselor here told me he remembers his father acting as I did and his Dad gave it to God and received counseling and his wife forgave him, after he raped his daughter which I never did. Today their marriage is the best one he knows of.

Judi, I wrote this letter several hours ago and I have been sitting here watching the sun go down through the bars of my window of my little room and I have been thinking deeply. I plead with you to see the great future we could have together with a willing attitude and God's help. You are the one who taught me when I was an athiest about God's love and forgiveness and how nothing was impossible with God and I believed you all the way.

We both know also that divorce is never God's perfect plan but His perfect plan is for the marriage partners to be loving, compassionate, forgiving one another and not to let anger or bitterness destroy the marriage.

Love, Larry

My lawyer sent the following information to me, and I quote from a letter written by my husband's lawyer:

> *"I might add that I have been contacted by my client's mother and she is willing to assume responsibility for her son in New Jersey. I would suggest that perhaps this be the best solution to the problem. When he is released from the Lincoln Regional Center that by agreement he be allowed to leave and go to his mother's home in New Jersey. If you have any other questions or comments, do not hesitate to get in touch with me."*

Bitterness fought for control of my heart as I read about the latest course of events. My husband was to be released from the mental hospital and, by court ruling, was permitted to return to his mother in New Jersey. Meanwhile, we, the victims, were continuing to live by the dictates of the court, engaged in weekly counseling sessions. The police and Social Services had open access to our home anytime of the day and night for the next year. I knew that we desperately needed the help, but it seemed so unfair. Larry would be with his mother for Christmas, while I was bound to reside in Nebraska and legally not permitted to go home to mine because we lived under protective supervision of the court.

I had to get permission to go across town to shop. Larry left the State free of restrictions, other than being responsible to support our girls, which he never did. After careful reflection on Larry's letter, I wrote the following:

Larry:

I guess I should have written this letter a long time ago but I kept thinking I would feel better if I waited. Well, I feel worse. I just don't understand how you could say you love me when you have hurt me so badly. I really hate you and the life I live because of you. I wish I had shot you with the shotgun the night Debbie told me and then I could have gone to jail and when they let me out I could start over somewhere knowing you would never hurt us again.

How could you do this to us after all we did for you? It really hurts to know I wasted 18 years of my life on a jerk like you and was too blind and trusting to know the difference. I really hate myself, almost as much as I do you. I wish you had committed suicide one of the many times you threatened to and then I could be free of you and your painful hold on my life. There aren't enough ugly words to express how badly and deeply hurt we all are over your selfish and stupid acts. I have tried to keep quiet and not to make too much fuss but you see I just can't get over how deep and searing the pain is. Every time one of the girls has a problem or is a problem, I hate you all over again. I am sick of hating you. I almost wish I were dead.

Thanks for nothing, Judi

Looking back it's easier to assess one's actions. However, at that time I was incapable of any communication with Larry. His acceptance of me was always contingent upon my passing his tests and fulfilling his conditions and needs. I had experienced more failure than success. In the experience of repeated failure there was conflict, fear, frustration, pain and ultimately some form of self-hatred. I tried to assume an appearance of pleasing Larry to gain living acceptance. I gave up on being myself and tried to be someone else, someone who was worthy of his recognition and love.

I could easily trace Larry's obnoxious behavior to the invisible roots of an unsuccessful struggle for self-esteem, until he hurt me. The desire for self-preservation forced me to stop trying to understand him and I found I wanted to judge and even hurt him.

There must be a constant intake of reassurance from the love of others. When I found myself without love or recognition of my own worth, I felt empty and bankrupt. I hurt very deeply, but this pain, unlike any other, didn't tell me what to do about it. If I touched a very hot object, the pain would tell me to pull away. But the pain of self-hatred and worthlessness is harder to understand and interpret. It's almost an unconscious pain.

The very thing that I was so reluctant to concede to Larry was in fact my greatest need: true love and appreciation. Self-doubt and self-hatred were the common cancers that ravished, distorted and destroyed our relationship and trust.

The Curse

Daydreams sometimes eased my loneliness and I wondered what would it be like to have a man spontaneously say "I love you!"

I don't know I had never experienced it. I read books about how it felt to be special. I wondered what it was like to anticipate his return in the evening or to believe that he was the best man in the world. I was a stranger to any such experiences.

Sin comes in many sizes and shapes, such as thoughts, for example.

Trish once openly said, "Why can't God let Dad die in a car accident and cease this torment?"

It was a good question. I agreed mentally. That is sin, at least it was for me and I knew it. Larry was like an abnormal child. He was my lot in life. Guilt plagued me for years because I did not love him as I should and he never showed any kindness to me.

Things were backward. I'd desperately pray for more love and he'd use it up in two days. I'd be left empty, begging God again. For years I was upset and unhappy with Larry, and he was probably just as upset with me.

The Bible says divorce is permissible for one reason, adultery! For years I believed Larry was a faithful husband to me, so my natural conclusion to my unhappiness was my fault.

As a preacher's wife I had counselled other women who'd been physically abused by their husbands. I didn't tell them to stay in a situation where their physical life was endangered. Could I tell myself to stay in a situation where my mental and emotional life was endangered, where my self-esteem was nonexistent? I live in frustration and dejection. I prayed hours a day just to be able to keep treading water to keep from drowning. The preacher was my husband. You don't speak against the man of God. The Bible say in Psalm 105:15:

> *"Touch not my annointed and do my prophets no harm."*

I had to be careful. I knew God's Presence had been on Larry in the beginning of his ministry, and yet I knew that I couldn't live with him and stay sane. One day I read a magazine article by Jamie Buckingham about divorced ministers. He said, "The church has to learn that they are people, too; not to be exiled, but loved."

I also knew during those years that I could never be happy with Larry but couldn't divorce him. The Bible didn't allow it. Self-hate told me I was hiding behind scripture.[1] I didn't want to be a divorced woman. I didn't want to live in hell, either. I wasn't raised by godly parents to be driven insane by a man who couldn't cope with life or me.

Larry wrote several letters from the hospital begging me to give God a second chance to work a miracle in our marriage. I realized that his idea of a miracle and mine were as far apart as the East is from the West. My idea of a miracle was being free of him.

Counseling taught me a lot. I started to think clearly and began to recover from the awful blow Larry had dealt us. I became free from the mental and emotional oppression and knew that to ask him back would be asking for death. I was seeking freedom from condemnation and the freedom of not having to be responsible for the one who was ordained to be responsible for me. My freedom also meant being able to make up my mind to do something and do it. It was so nice to be free and yet I really wasn't free. The Scriptures and Biblical principles that I had been taught confused me. I felt like a haunted woman. Everytime I spoke to people they didn't seem surprised that I would divorce my husband, but when they realized he was a preacher suddenly they acted like I was a fallen woman.

"You were a preacher's wife? You want to be divorced?" I was made to feel that I was committing the unpardonable sin.

---

[1] Matthew 5:32, Mark 10:4

The Lord was feeding me and I was growing spiritually. I believed God could do something with my life.

Then somebody would come up and say, "You were a preacher's wife? You divorced a preacher?" It would send me plummeting to the bottom once more to begin the steep ascent back to sanity alone.

The religious magazines I read all told me divorce was wrong and that it wasn't God's plan. In my heart of hearts I knew it certainly was not His perfect will. I also knew that living with Larry meant being in torment continually and that wasn't God's plan for me, either. I had been the legal head of our household for the last few years. I knew I was going to have a hard time raising these children without a daddy, but I'd also had a hard time raising them with a daddy.

Counselors gave me statistics of success stories of reunited families, but they never talked about the children five or six years later, or even 10 years later to see how they turned out. The wives weren't asked about the hard times after the husband's return. No one wanted to talk about it. Or perhaps it was because the program was too new to really assess the situation properly.

Larry's mother wrote and told me how much Larry loved me and said that I should take him back. He needed me, she said. I knew he needed me, but he needed a caretaker even more. He told his mother the same old line, that I was not giving God a chance to work a miracle in our marriage.

I said to myself, "But my miracle is here, I'm free!" How much more of a miracle could I want? But bitterness filled my life. Everytime I thought about divorce, I cried myself to sleep.

A week before the divorce was finalized, I talked to a lady who went to our church. Her husband had been a minister with a personality disorder and she finally divorced him. She told me that he had driven her to distraction to the point that she sought help from a psychiatrist, because she was convinced that she was ill. About a year after they divorced, her husband committed suicide. It broke me up because I knew that Larry had threatened suicide. I understood that she was still healing from the years of marital abuse and his suicide.

I knew that Larry might commit suicide, but I forced myself to remember that it was his problem.

The question that haunted me was, "Why can't I be free? Why can't the court let me be free? Why can't God let me be free?"

A Christian friend wrote a long letter reminding me that our marriage vows were "until death do us part" and I had no business breaking them.

That was the straw that broke the camel's back.

I called her and said, "You don't realize what you have asked me to do, because of what he did to my children, and the hell we all lived in."

She answered me by quoting scriptures. I told her that the State of Nebraska had unbound me and all the devils in hell couldn't tie me up again.

I was furious.

"Until you can face my girls and tell them that what their father did to them was right, when it wasn't, you have nothing to say to any of us," I told her.

I had known the Lord since I was a child. I knew that He wanted what was best for all of us. I knew this pain wasn't His perfect will and I also knew that He didn't like divorce but I knew that He loved me. I was not going to be told what to do by somebody who was self-righteous. God had worked a miracle in my life, delivering me from the hell of Larry and from his condemnation.

The day that the divorce was final, I called Larry and we talked for about 30 minutes. I told him I was sorry. I knew that he didn't understand. I reminded him that he was free to do anything he pleased, because I was not responsible for him anymore. He cried and begged me to take him back and threatened suicide. I told him it was too late and hung up.

Weeping, I sank to my knees on the floor and cried. Then I felt the whole weight of responsibility for Larry fall off of my shoulders. But my soul remained in the grip of bitterness and hate. I knew that I wasn't doing what society and the church expected of a preacher's wife. It was the step that I had dared to take, and I was blessed to some degree. But I was left absolutely alone and lonely.

The girls and I celebrated the divorce by going out for dinner. Knowing that I had chosen them did more to cement our relationship than any other single thing. For the first time in years both Debbie and Trish began to trust me. Eventually that trust reached out to include their Heavenly Father as well.

During this time, I was trying to hang onto my faith. I was praying and we were attending church. But my real attitude was one of anger. I simply didn't understand how God could have allowed this to happen. My confusion was compounded by those who believe that a real Christian would not have to go through something as dreadful as this.

Depression engulfed both Trish and me. She looked so pathetic, locked up, and talked very little. Sometimes at night I dreamed that Larry was back and touching the girls again.

Debbie ran away a couple of times and was an increasing problem. My girls were angry at Larry, then God, me and finally each other. What a broken little band we were. This is the curse the Bible speaks of in Malachi 4:6. Broken marriages breed broken children.

When the girls finished their school year I decided I would like to move back home and received the court's permission to do so. Debbie said she wouldn't go with us and ran away again. Finally she returned and we left together for my parents' loving home and hearts. Healing began in a significant way between us that summer.

With the help of Christian friends I finally started putting the past behind me and setting new goals for myself. Our pastor spent much time just listening to me and the girls and helped us greatly. His caring attitude demonstrated the love of Christ and presented the girls with an excellent example of what to look for in an adult male.

The love of the Lord reached both the girls and they simultaneously began to forgive and let go of the past. They were far ahead of me in that respect. Faith isn't really faith until it's all you have. I realized that it was all I had. Carefully I started to believe God with renewed joy, and in myself again.

CHOOSE LIFE

"We are free now," I kept telling myself, "free to live!" Nebraska was far behind us. The girls had grown tall and lovely, one dark and vivacious, the other blonde and beautiful.

Good things were happening in our lives.

In October, 1984, I decided that I would go back to college and study to become a nurse. When I received my Licensed Practical Nurse degree, for the first time in years I was pleased with myself. I had also become actively involved in a church where I played the organ.

Throughout my high school years, God and I had a working relationship. Although it wasn't that deep, He did keep me from several disasters.

During the years with Larry, living through one crisis after another, I developed a relationship of hanging on with God. I guess when the crisis came I just got tired of holding on and collapsed into God's arms. God was good. I knew that the life of faith was a possibility. I knew that it could work.

Now I longed to get above the survival level and to be an overcomer. But the hate still lingered.

I read a book on anger and tried to release it. I asked God to forgive me and I felt he had. But down deep I nursed a sore spot I couldn't get rid of. When someone touched it I just fell apart.

My counselor once told me that Larry couldn't hurt me unless I let him. But I kept allowing him access to my soul. I could hardly go weeks without spending at least a day in depression. Something the kids would say or do, memories, a snide remark, even a kindness, and I'd disintegrate.

I knew I had to get over it and I had to stop allowing Larry to hurt me. The million-dollar question was, "How?"

One summer the girls and I went to a youth camp. They enjoyed it. I was the camp cook. Both Trish and Debbie received sound, loving Biblical counsel at the camp. For the first time they began to share openly with me things Larry had said and done. I listened as Trish, curled up at the foot of my bed, expressed the agony she had locked away.

She explained it like this:

"Because I carried the stain of what I was as a child and I buried who I was, hid it from everyone, I needed a lot of help. My counselor explained that the Holy Spirit had to take a 'scrub brush' to the wounded area within me in order to remove the tough scabs that had formed there over the years. The Lord had to get down to the bottom of the wound before the healing process could permanently begin."

Trish showed me Isaiah 1:18 from her Open Bible, reading aloud:

"Come now and let us reason together, saith the Lord, though your sins be as scarlet, they shall be as white as snow; though they be red like crimson they shall be as wool."

"The next step, my counselor told me, was forgiveness," Trish said. "I asked my Heavenly Father to help me forgive my parents for what they did to me. Then I repented and asked Him to forgive me for the bitterness I harbored against you and Dad for so long. Another heavy burden was lifted from my shoulders: the Holy Spirit helped me to see that I bore no responsibility for what had happened, that I had never been to blame and had no reason to feel ashamed. I could hardly believe it at first because I'd been demented by guilt.

"I learned to identify with Jesus' blood sacrifice for my sin. God abhors sin but Jesus took my curse when He died and I sure don't understand how it works but I'm free now. I asked the Father in Jesus' name to plant my life in that blood sacrifice and to protect me from my parents and He did. The hurt and fear both left and Jesus is my defense, my protecter. Mom, you can't hurt me and Dad can't destroy me anymore. Now I'm learning to live a new resurrection life by literally eating the Word of God and feeding my famished mind and spirit."

Her shining, crystal-clear countenance attested to the fact that something very significant had taken place. Trish, known at home as the quiet one, certainly was open that night.

Trish continued: "The relief I experience every day is indescribable. I know I am right with God again, I feel clean, forgiven and loved by Him. And, what's more, I'm willing to believe in His love for me. It's taken me awhile but that's why I came Mom, to tell you!" She hugged me. I was surprised by my lack of joy for her. She was experiencing a deliverance from pain I knew nothing about.

Debbie slipped into my cabin on several occasions that same summer, for the Lord was breaking through to her as well.

One day she told me, "I tried to suppress the memories of the past, but on occasion they surfaced, in flashbacks. I was a master at pushing them out of sight again. Hurt and shame sat just beneath the surface of my life like a cancer in my soul, an incurable wound. You know how it colored every area of my life, even my relationship with God.

"But how could I trust my Heavenly Father when my earthly father had all but destroyed my mental and emotional stability? This burden made me defensive and fearful of being hurt again. I became critical, a perfectionist, hard on myself and harder still on those closest to me. Deep down I felt like an outcast, a leper."

I listened quietly as Debbie very dramatically and graphically described her condition and tried not to betray the alarming truth that she was also painting a picture of my own condition.

"My Christian counselor asked me to verbalize my feelings, to tell the Lord about the shame, anger, frustration, and bitterness I had kept inside," said Debbie rapidly. "I was not aware of how strong these feelings were that I battled. I was exhausted by the intensity of my emotions and flood of tears that issued from the accumulated years of dirt and hurt. At times I felt nauseous and vomited up phlegm."

She paused for a moment, then continued, "With the knowledge that I was acceptable to God through my faith in the Lord Jesus I received the insight and ability to fight off the smothering sense of guilt. I will call it false, because that's what it is. I put away forever the idea that I brought all this misery upon myself. I was a child and a victim. It was not my fault! I was not to blame for the wrong choices of my parents. My dad's choice to abuse me was just that — his own wrong choice. Someone more trustworthy would not have taken advantage of me no matter how tempting the situation.

"Jesus knows what it's like to suffer innocently and unjustly. What would we do without the Lord to heal us?" Then she quoted Psalm 62:8:

> "Trust in Him at all times, O people, pour out your heart before Him; God is a refuge for us."

Debbie's defensive attitude toward me had vanished and she spoke to me as an equal. "I was in a mess and not just because Dad molested me, but because I refused to forgive him," she said. "Unforgiveness kept me a slave to my past and opened the door for mental torment, just like Jesus said:

> "So also My Heavenly Father will deal with anyone of you, if you do not freely forgive your brother from your heart for his offense."

"I know that I wasn't responsible for the abuse that I suffered but I saw that I was responsible for my own sins of rebellion, hatred and bitterness which I had allowed to fill my life. I decided to forgive, it was a free-will choice, not because my dad needed it, which of course he did, but because I needed it. It's true Dad didn't deserve forgiveness but none of us do for that matter. Forgiveness is a gift. If you want to be healed from the wrong that's been done to you, you must learn to forgive!"

"Debbie," I responded, because my daughter had taken the very step that I was not yet willing to take, the one of unconditional forgiveness, "I'm happy for you dear."

That summer the sad truth is that my girls grew emotionally while I remained warped.

Male companionship was something I had only read about until I met John. We were both in the church choir and became friends at rehearsal breaks. I told him that I was rearing two teenagers alone but was careful not to disclose why. He said that his 17-year-old daughter was taking drugs and his wife ran out on him and divorced him. At that point I told him about our break up but reserved all of the sordid details. His only comment was very disconcerting when he asked, "Are you sure that you had nothing to do with the break up of your home and marriage?"

I was surprised by his forthrightness and responded with a quick, "No!"

Later, alone, the only reason that I could think of for our divorce was Larry's sexual abuse of the girls. I was very careful to tell John later that I had done all there was to do and I quite frankly believed it with all of my heart.

John, was a courteous person, easy to be with, and I was comfortable with our relationship. He treated me like a lady and it unnerved me. But I genuinely was thrilled by his kindness shown in so many ways, such as opening the door for me.

One day he called me early and we went out for coffee and a chat after Wednesday service. From then our visits became regular, a couple of times a week. He helped my parents with odd jobs in the house, endearing himself to us all. He spoke words that built faith. He was living in a kind of victory which made my level of bare survival all the more apparent to me.

"Out of the abundance of the heart the mouth speaketh," he'd quote Jesus' words.

Unconsciously I spewed forth tirades of doubt and unbelief but I felt convicted. In spite of John's verbalizing the Word of God, I found myself irresistibly fighting against him and it shocked me because I was a Christian.

Everytime he took me out to dinner, or stopped to buy something for me, I became guilt-ridden. Finally I realized that I had been a fool for too long.

Once he said to me, "You are impossible." He was correct!

John was especially supportive of my attempts to be a godly mother and he was sensitive to the girls' problems. However, our dating created some problems at first because the girls, especially Debbie, were jealous of any new relationship that I might develop with a man. They felt threatened by a new father image.

John caused me to re-evaluate my life.

Everyone, he told me, is born with unique and unconditional values but we can only know ourselves as reflected in the eyes of others. I hadn't heard this kind of teaching before.

"Judi," John asked, "have you really tried to see and affirm your own unconditional and unique value? Do you really try to consider and fulfill your needs? Have you really forgiven yourself for your faults and mistakes? Think about it. Do you think of yourself as genuine and loving as you do others in your life, whom you love the most? Do you offer someone else the same kind of warmth and understanding that you offer yourself?"

He paused for a moment, then added, "Do you know true and realistic self-esteem is the basic element in the health of all human personality? People act and relate to other people in accordance with the way they think or feel about themselves!"

Shocked silence filled the space between us. I couldn't begin to answer any of his provocative questions so I just cried in pathetic self-pity.

Slowly, however, my own needs began to make sense. Instead of getting up in the middle of the night to get Larry a glass of water I should have said, "Get yourself one." I was wrong not to insist that he open the door for me, that he take out the trash, that he do all the things that husbands are to do to lighten the load. I was wrong to have been his full-time servant. My mistake was I couldn't take the risk of his doing it wrong so I did it for him. I had a very hard time dealing with myself and admitting my lack of self love.

When I was still a nursing student, we went shopping one afternoon. John was looking at stereos and I at stethoscopes. I chose one that fit my student budget. To my surprise he joined me and took an interest in my choice.

He picked another one up and said, "What about this?" I explained that it was large and heavy.

He looked at the one in my hand and took it up to the sales clerk and said, "I'll take it." I was speechless and embarrassed. I didn't know what to say.

I couldn't remember Larry ever saying, "Why don't we buy this?" It was always, "Take care of it, Judi." If I needed it, I planned, saved, budgeted and then went out and got it.

I had to fight to keep myself from saying to John, "Well I didn't plan, or budget."

I experienced a great conflict of emotions. I was pleased John cared enough to buy the stetho- scope but self-hate rose up — knowing I had put up with so little for so long. It almost overwhelmed me.

We got into the car and I asked, "Why does it hurt so much when someone treats me nicely?" I fought back the tears. When I got home I cried and hated myself all over again. Although I worked really hard at it I just couldn't keep the lid on my runaway emotions. I was reacting to everything. My life was an ache that seemed fathomless.

John never had a bad day and I hardly ever had a good one. He was the first man I ever found it easy to pray with and he was the first ever to pray for me. Larry always went to the study to pray and if I needed something, I prayed for it myself.

One day John put his hands on my shoulders and smiled into my tear-filled eyes and said, "Let's pray a prayer of faith today, OK?" It felt so good.

The girls and I were living at mother's. One day I was in the kitchen making John a snack. I told him how hard it was for me to live at home.

"Let's pray," he said.

He started to pray right there in the kitchen and the Lord reassured me that he had a purpose for my life. That had never happened to me before and I had been married to a minister for years. Here God was speaking to me right in my own kitchen.

Larry prayed for everyone else but never for me. When Larry preached he looked right past me because I was only his slave.

It felt so good to be ministered to. I was reassured having an adequate, handsome, financially independent man of God around. He was an answer to my prayers because I needed a friend. I hadn't prayed for a husband because I was afraid that I would be in bondage again.

John was always willing to minister to me. A true friend, he was concerned. God answered his prayers for the girls and me. He encouraged us to have faith. Slowly I began to realize that this living in the Lord, this faith life, was within the scope of my being, instead of just looking at it from afar.

Our relationship developed on a friendship basis until we drove several hours one weekend to attend a concert. We discussed various Biblical topics, listened to tapes, and laughed like a couple of kids. I just enjoyed it all and felt so cared for. On the way home I drove and John slept. I couldn't ever remember sleeping on a trip with Larry. I'd be as tense as a cat either driving or calling directions and making all of the decisions.

John awoke. I pulled over and he took the wheel. About an hour from home I started to cry.

He put his arm around me and said, "What's the matter, Judi?"

I couldn't tell him. I just sat there and cried for the lost years of my life. I realized that I had lived below the level of reasonableness for too long. I had trouble in believing in John's kindness to me. It was too good to be true. I ached and the pain seemed to envelop me. John took me home and kissed me goodnight.

Through the months I was able to open up to John and tell him something of what life had been like with Larry. He knew him from photographs and I volunteered the information that he was living in a room at the YMCA and working as a night security guard.

Winter had come, snow was blowing outside and we were at home by the cozy fireside. John casually mentioned, "Judi there is something you should know. I have been to seminary, am a graduate and was a minister."

My heart fell.

I'd vowed I would never date a preacher. "John," I said, sliding away from him, "I'd never marry a preacher again."

Later in my room I cried because I knew this was the end of our friendship. My father said to me the next morning, "Are you going to scratch him off of your list, Judi?"

"Yes, Daddy."

Not that my list was long, it wasn't. Do not misunderstand me, John was a fine Christian man and the presence of the Lord in his life was very evident to everyone with whom he came in contact. People were encouraged and helped everywhere he went. But he was a preacher. I had no emotional strength to handle that.

John gathered courage to tell me he loved me.

"We have to stop this relationship, John," I told him. "We have to break it off! I'm of no use to anybody, not even God." I was not emotionally strong enough to enter into another marriage at that stage.

One night John came back to the house and announced to both Debbie and Trish, "I saw your father on Friday night!"

That did it! The girls stormed out and looked at me as if I was Judas Iscariot himself.

"John how could you?" I asked, getting angry. "I'm sorry I'm upset but you have no right to talk to the girls about their father."

He said, "I love you!"

I just broke into tears.

"John, I've committed my life to my children who have been terribly hurt. I'm not capable or ready to trust my life to anybody else except God. Please take your hands off of my life. Be nice to somebody else! I don't think it's possible to love anybody enough to be hurt again."

Quietly he said, "Judi you've never forgiven Larry, have you?"

"Yes I have, because I knew if I didn't God wouldn't hear my prayers," I said. "He hurt me so long ago before the girls were even born and I don't think that I've forgiven him for that."

"Why did you marry Larry?"

"He said he would commit suicide if I didn't."

"You never forgave him for that, either?"

I knew that I hadn't. I stood there sobbing. John walked across the room, put his arms around me and wept with me.

After a while he said, "Judi, you have to get it straight, you know that. Just ask him to forgive you. You have to reconcile."

"We've been divorced two years," I explained. "There is no such thing as reconciliation for this."

"But there can be for you," he gently insisted.

I didn't want John to get into the middle of my pain to see how badly it really hurt.

"John you just don't understand, I can't handle you butting into this! Its been good to have you for a friend but I'm too proud to get close to another man. It hurts me everytime I think about Larry and the hate comes back and I can't handle it."

I don't ever remember anybody caring enough about me to cry. I knew that John was honest with me by showing me that as a proud woman I was having a hard time touching the Lord. I was letting hate and bitterness for Larry block me from God's presence. I didn't want this friend to know how much I hated Larry. I guess I didn't even want to believe that God knew the depth of my hatred. But I couldn't stop him from finding out.

"Just go to Larry and ask him to forgive you," John said.

Then I knew down deep inside he was right.

But I couldn't do it.

"You are 90 percent of the way home and all that's left to do is to ask Larry to forgive you."

I wanted the pain to go but I was scared. I was afraid that Larry wouldn't accept my apology.

"It isn't your place to make the terms of acceptance, it is only your place to confess," John said.

I wept some more and he hugged me and said, "We're going to pray about this."

Then he said, "You have to forgive your children, too."

"They hated me so much in the past."

"I know, but you have to forgive and start the procedure so that God will have a chance to work things out."

"I can't."

"You have to, Judi."

I knew he was right.

"Judi, I'm going to pray about this but you need to see Larry, too."

"Yes," a voice spoke through me, "I will."

John got up and left me there to think things through. I sat alone with my God. Finally we had reached a point to let the lid come off. For 19 years I had carried hatred against Larry for the way he had manipulated me and not cared for me as a husband.

The filth began to come out as my life was relived before me. The Holy Spirit went to work bringing it up out of the depths of my being. I acknowledged my ugly response. I wasn't hiding anymore or pretending it wasn't so. I repented before a holy God. Dark, slimy failures to forgive were brought to the surface of my mind for acknowledgement by my will. I forgave until I couldn't think of more to forgive. A quiet but sure sense of freedom came and took up sentinel duty where the hatred and fears had been for years. I was weak, undone, naked in every way — but stronger than I had ever been. I was no man's debtor now.

I managed to go to nursing school the following morning.

Emotionally I felt like a basket case but my spirit was stronger.

Tuesday evening John called and said, "Judi, I went down to the YMCA and found Larry today. He wants to see you."

"I'll only go under one condition and that is I must have a third party."

"That's good, I'll be there," he assured me.

The appointment was made for a Sunday afternoon in one of the Sunday school rooms at a local church. Larry, John and I sat down at the table. I could see the fear in Larry's eyes.

He said, "Hi, Judi, I'm in great shape and God is blessing me."

"What a pathetic man," I thought.

"Larry, I am here to ask you to forgive me for hating you, and for holding —" I began hesitantly, "bitterness and resentment in my heart against you." I paused momentarily, then continued. "Larry, I hated and resented you. Please forgive me for all of the times I failed as your wife and wasn't what I should have been. Forgive me for all the times that I put up with situations when I should have gotten them straight and not wallowed in self-pity. I did the best that I could. I believe God gave me permission to divorce you.

"Larry, I'm sorry that it doesn't suit you but I feel it is right. I cannot live under your condemnation or that of anybody else anymore. Do you understand, Larry?"

"I'm getting used to living alone, learning to survive," he said, avoiding looking at me. "But, Judi, you really aren't giving God a chance to work a miracle in our marriage. Why didn't you listen and come to visit me in the hospital? Everything would have been just fine."

He had said exactly the same thing to me years ago at the police station. I was sorry.

I had repented, but my heart was broken afresh.

"Larry, you don't understand. This is God's miracle for me," I said.

"If you had listened to me, you'd have given God a chance to work a miracle in our marriage."

"No, I gave Him a chance to work a bigger miracle in my life."

Larry did not understand and I was truly frustrated, but God gave me His peace.

"Larry, do you realize that Judi has a legal and Biblical reason for divorcing you?" John asked.

"Well, I can see where legally she did but I don't think she was justified and I didn't do anything that would make her want to divorce me."

"Larry, are you still so angry?" John asked.

"Yes, I wrote her a letter and tried to get her to come across to my way of thinking. She shouldn't have done it. It's all her fault. She should have taken me back home." He spoke with a monotone.

"Do you realize she had that right?" John asked.

"Well she had a right to, but I asked her not to. She didn't give God a chance to work a miracle in our marriage!" he repeated.

"Larry, the girls are still hurting because of your treatment. It would be good if you could show them some real love, some manifestation just to show that you care," John advised.

"Well, Judi knows, I just don't make enough money."

I knew he worked part-time as a security guard because he couldn't handle a full-time job.

"Larry, I know that, but you need to tell the girls that you care," I told him.

"Larry, you need to be a father to your girls, even if it means doing something small," John said. "They need to know that their father is there and he cares."

"I don't make enough money," he insisted.

The conversation went downhill from there.

God broke through. By the confession of my mouth I was set free when I was willing to honestly face Larry. God took the hatred away. I felt so free I could have gotten up and danced. But I didn't because it wasn't appropriate under the circumstances. I felt the terrible weight lift off of my chest and I knew that bitterness was gone. God reconciled me to Himself through repentance and the confession of my mouth and forgiveness in my heart.

Now there was liberty in my spirit, freedom in my soul, and a peace in my heart that the world couldn't take away. I was no longer condemned by divorce. I had found the compassionate side to it. There is a liberty in it and God set me free. The peace didn't leave. Life is just as hard. But the peace of God is real and I can keep walking on. All of these years I suffered because of my unforgiveness and the compassionate side of divorce escaped me.

It is so wonderful to walk in freedom after years of condemnation and tears. There is no way that I can express how good it feels. I thank God for John because he made me face my true state of unforgiveness. I was afraid of Larry because of the fear and hatred in me but now I don't have any reason to wonder if he is going to be around the next corner. There is no reason for him to hurt me because I harbor no hate, bitterness or fear. I thank God for the freedom of forgiveness.

The power of forgiveness began to have an effect in Debbie's and Trish's lives. They picked out a church of their own on the other side of town and became actively involved in the choir there.

Months later they invited me to attend a musical entitled "Beyond Imagination" put on by the teens. To my amazement and joy they both sang solos. I knew they meant the words that they were singing. That night I was just another face in the audience but I was so moved I could hardly breathe. Like a medicine, the music and words of this production covered areas of concern that I had carried for my girls. They sang about how the love of God reached them "beyond imagination." I felt a little proud of myself and I was very proud of God and them. It was a little measure of success for all of us.

I persisted in school and today am an operating room nurse. My two girls are grown up. Trish has graduated from high school, has lots of friends, and seems well-adjusted. She is preparing for college.

Debbie graduated from high school and joined the Air Force. She met a fine young man and fell in love. She sent me this card and note at Christmas:

Hello Mother:

Just a short Christmas greeting to tell you I'm lonely and miss you lots. I never before realized how homesickness seems to sneak up and before you know it, you have a wad of Kleenexes and runny nose that seems to trickle the rest of the day.

My first Christmas away from home and my one and only marriage coming up. It's hard to believe that in three days I'll be Mrs. Richard Short. You're going to love your new son-in-law. He's just so adorable, it's incredible. I never thought anyone could ever love me as much as he does. He's something I've waited for all my life. God is working everything out for us. I love you and everyone. Mother, I'll be home to see you soon enough with Richard. One day

there will be a new addition to your family.
Think you could handle being a grandma? I
know for a fact I can handle being a mother.
                              Love, Debbie

Larry still doesn't understand what he did. He thinks I should take him back. He sends me a Mother's Day card every year and tells me that he is right with God. But still he shows no signs of repentance. I don't think he has ever told the girls that he is sorry. He has never shown a great deal of interest in their welfare. They are still angry at times because of his total lack of support.

Three and a half years after our divorce, Larry gave 16-year-old Trish a Christmas gift of bath salts and powder. It cost $15.95. The gift consisted of three identical boxes with two naked ladies on each box. Trish was immediately sickened and returned it to the store to choose something more appropriate.

Last spring she saw him in line behind her at the Burger King. She'd cut her hair and wore make-up. He didn't recognize her, but she was aware of him and quickly gave her money to a girlfriend and said, "Buy what I want, I'll get us a table."

The girls sat outside at a picnic table. It was about 10 p.m. after a young people's meeting at the church. Lights were strung up outside giving a bright, cheery effect. Larry got his burger and went to his car. As he drove by the girls, he stopped, leaned out of the window and said, "Do you need anything? Can I take you any place?"

"I have to laugh at it because there's so much to cry about," Trish commented. "I've seen him just once or twice and I feel this strange tingling start in my toes and move up my legs, making its way through those tight knots in my stomach and then what could have been hatred melts into pity. I feel sorry for him and sorry for myself that it ever happened. I am without a father."

Looking back, it has been a long, rocky road. I'm so grateful for the counseling services the Nebraska courts provided. My eyes were opened to the plight of so many others hurt by incest.

However, I must give honor to whom it is due. The unconditional love of the Lord has turned our mourning into dancing. He has taken the ashes of our burned-out lives and returned His beauty. This is a miracle the magnitude of which no doctor, social worker or psychologist is capable.

When our Heavenly Father comes on the scene He begins in the spirit, and keeps right on working his cleansing power out through the soul and into the body.

Yom Kippur, the Day of Atonement, is the most sacred day of the Jewish faith. In Biblical times, on this day of fasting and penitence, the High Priest solemnly entered into the Holy of Holies, in the great Temple of Jerusalem petitioning the Almighty to forgive the sins of the Jewish nation. He was seeking their forgiveness.

At some point throughout the 24-hour-long fast, today observant Jews repeat the following prayer. We Christians would do well to take note:

> *"We have turned away from your*
> *wonderful mitzvos,*
> *And now we see that we gained*
> *nothing.*

> *And you are the just One, regarding any*
>   *punishment that befalls us.*
> *For your actions are truthful and we*
>   *have wickedly sinned.*
> *What can we say before you,*
> *Whose seat is so elevated; and what can*
>   *we tell you,*
> *Who dwells in the heavens.*
> *For all that is hidden, all that is*
>   *revealed, you know.*
> *You know never-revealed secrets and*
>   *the secrets of every individual.*
> *You search all of the chambers of the*
>   *stomach[1] and examine the kidneys[2]*
>   *and the heart[3]*
> *There is nothing hidden to you, there is*
>   *nothing secret from before your eyes.*
> *And for all of these, God of forgiveness,*
>   *forgive us, pardon us, cleanse us."[4]*

After long, empty years, I found release from bitterness and hatred. Our prayers were heard and we all experienced new depths of divine forgiveness. What a delightful surprise it was some time later to welcome my first grandson into this world, born on the Day of Atonement.

---

[1] Symbolizing all of the physical causes of sin.
[2] Which gives counsel to the heart.
[3] Which carries out its counselor's advice, symbolizing the corrupting of the mind
[4] Viduy, pgs. 22, 23, 26.

ABBA FATHER

"And He shall turn the heart of the fathers to the children, and the heart of the children to their fathers, lest I come and smite the earth with a curse," Malachi 4:6.

This statement of fact is given specifically to fathers. We knew something of the curse mentioned here. The four of us were living out the results of a broken, violated love relationship. We were reaping the fruit of destructive seed which was rooted in Larry's misconceived attitudes concerning the character of Father God.

Thus, my girls not only were robbed of a secure, loving, natural father but just as important they were blocked from a true understanding of their Heavenly Father. Larry and I were robbed as well.

Today the greatest need in the world is for restoration of broken relationships. Statistics point out the systematic destruction of marriage and the home in this generation. A direct result is the sky-rocketing increase in sexual abuse of children.[1] This work of restoration must begin in the home.

The prophet Malachi dealt with this issue of fathers and children when penning the very last words of the Old Testament. With awesome prophetic finality he proclaims God's judgment for the misrepresentation of true fatherhood by "lest I come and smite the earth with a curse."

Today one doesn't have to look far for the curse: pornography, the battered wife, abortion, homosexuality with its accompanying acquired immune deficiency syndrome, the battered child, the missing child, divorce, drugs and alcohol are so ingrained into the fabric of our society that we barely lift an eyebrow anymore. The sacred trust of the father-child relationship has been all but destroyed. Man has sown the wind and is reaping the whirlwind.

However, the promise is:

"He shall turn the hearts of the fathers ..."

This promise feeds hope into man's hopelessness. God is able to turn the heart of the fathers to the children. This turning involves a change of attitude, repentance. Before the fall Adam trusted God. After the fall he trusted himself; and mistrusted or rejected God's companionship. Man sets himself up as a self-centered, final authority by his own words, "I will." This rejection of God is the

---

[1] Little Ones, Inc.

cause of rebellion which begins a process of self-rejection, rejection of others, aloneness and isolation, resulting in autism. Self-rejection is highlighted in perverse sexual relationships as described in the first chapter of the book of Romans:

"And so, since they did not see fit to acknowledge or approve of Him or consider Him worth the knowing, God gave them over to a base and condemned mind to do things not proper or decent but loathsome," Romans 1:28. (Amplified New Testament)

In the book of Genesis, 3:1-6, we read the story of the temptation and the fall. The big lie which the serpent got Eve to believe was that God would deprive her of something good, as if He hadn't already given her everything! It was the message of deprivation, the suggestion that she should mistrust God. There is a temptation to rebel through a wrong attitude about the very character and nature of God Himself.

Eve believed she was being cheated out of something good so she reached out and took the fruit for herself. Then having violated the principles set down by God, Adam blamed and abused his co-inheritor Eve. We read:

"The woman whom thou gavest to be with me, she gave me of the fruit and I did eat," Genesis 4:11b.

Man makes his own rules and grabs his own "goodies" which result in the dysfunctional family and damaged children.

Our misconception of God is our misconception of love, God is love!

> *"He who does not love has not become acquainted with God, and does not and never did know Him; for God is love,"* 1 John 4:8.

The greatest trial in life is to be deprived of father love. Many are born with an inherited sense of deprivation because of faulty love relationships at home which cause dysfunction. An opening is therefore formed in one's spirit, resulting in vulnerability which reinforces other weaknesses both spiritually and physically.

Job suffered great losses and blamed himself.

"I'm vile, I'm vile," he said.

He only changed his attitude when he saw himself as God saw him. Then he repented, for he was relating to Father God's unconditional love. He was totally dependent upon his Creator for the sense of well-being and purpose for living that he needed. Job not only repented, he forgave his "comforters." This then freed him and resulted in a mature, reciprocal relationship with God. God was there through it all, accepting and loving Job. With the realization of God's total, all-encompassing acceptance of himself, Job turned and responded to God's unconditional love. He knew he was accepted by his Heavenly Father. As proof let us read:

"For I know that my redeemer liveth and that he shall stand at the latter day upon the earth. And though worms destroy this body, in my flesh shall I see God," Job 19:25, 26.

Look at Lucifer's attitude toward God. This prince who once headed the heavenly host in praises of the Almighty, this former beautiful created being, is responsible for the attitude of the heart that rejects the knowledge of God. He is a rejected being, cast out of Heaven by the Father. He decided to rebel against God's authority and began a process of self-hate and deprivation which is reproduced worldwide before our eyes.

The process of rebellion begins with the rejection of the knowledge of God, in one's will:

"How art thou fallen from Heaven, O Lucifer, son of the morning. Now art thou cut down to the ground, which didst weaken the nations. For thou hast said in thine heart, I will ascend into heaven, I will exalt my throne above the stars of God: I will sit also upon the mount of the congregation, in the side of the north; I will ascend above the heights of the clouds; I will be like the Most High!" Isaiah 14:12, 13, 14.

The good news is that Jesus was sent to lead us into a heart knowledge of the Father. His life, lived out in perfect accordance with the laws of God to the nation of Israel, expressed perfectly the heart of God the Father, calling, reconciling Israel, and the world to Himself. Yet, how many of us profess to know Jesus and are orphaned in our relationship to our Heavenly Father? Does it not reflect back to the relationship we had or didn't have with our natural fathers?

Continually Jesus turns us to our Heavenly Father's heart, the Father's plans and the Father's love for mankind.

> *"He is the rewarder of them who diligently seek Him," Heb. 11:6.*
>
> *"He will withhold nothing good from them who love Him and are the called according to His purpose," II Tim. 1:9.*
>
> *"We know that we are the called of God, not that we loved Him, but that He loved us and sent His Son to be the propitiation for our sins," I John 4:10.*

Continually the Bible teaches us that God the Father gave from the moment of creation until now. Therefore, when the natural father's relationship with his child is one of selfishness and abuse in any form, he inflicts a dark isolation upon that impressionable young soul, a self-loathing, that will remain forever unless it is divinely removed by the supernatural love of his Father God.

> *"So any person who knows what is right to do but does not do it, to him it is sin," James 4:17.*
>
> *"... whosoever causes one of these little ones who believes in Me to stumble, it is better for him that a heavy millstone be*

*hung around his neck, and that he be
drowned in the depth of the sea," Matt. 18:6.*

   *"See that you do not despise one of
these little ones, for I say to you, that their
angels in Heaven continually behold the
face of My Father who is in Heaven,"
Matt. 18:10.*

A child's concept of God as a Father becomes a
distortion of the truth because the sense of security
and trust and need for love were never met by the
natural father. According to the Biblical pattern, the
father is the source of love, not the mother. She
reflects his love.

Therefore sexual abuse is believed to be the
most damaging of all crimes. "These children don't
have broken bones, they have broken souls. What
really damages them is keeping it all bottled up."[2]

The Bible tells us that the body is the temple of
the Holy Spirit[3] to be shared with a mate in holi-
ness and honor, not in lust.[4] Sexual embrace is
never a physical union only; our entire person is
involved, willing or unwillingly. One cannot touch
the body and not affect the spirit living within.[5]

In marriage we are designed to become one
flesh in blessedness as God ordained.[6] To come together in any other way is defilement.[7] Sexual abuse

---

[2] Newsweek, August 9, 1986. "Acting Out A Secret," Ann
   Burgess.
[3] I Cor. 18-20
[4] I Thess. 4:3-6
[5] James 2:26
[6] Gen. 2:4
[7] Heb. 13:4

confuses identity, plants fear of being chosen, offers no promise of being cherished, and makes a girl wonder how God could allow such a horrible thing to happen. She is estranged, belonging to no one.

Who doesn't long in their hearts to change their depraved, twisted past? Like Gulliver, of *Gulliver's Travels,* we are strapped down by chords, immobile but longing for release. We cannot go back to the past but God can go back for us and heal us.

We must accept ourselves with the same compassion and unconditional love the Lord has for us. Then we will be able to present ourselves nakedly, trusting Him, acknowledging our sin.

He can heal the wounds and atrophied emotions irreparably damaged and cause us to live fully in the present, loving and being loved.

When the prodigal son was still far off, the Bible says his father went out to meet him. God's nature is one of reconciling the world to himself. His nature of redemptive love produces repentance on our part.

The Holy Spirit woos us and turns us to Jesus.

Jesus leads us on into cleansing for sin through his blood sacrifice, and turns us to begin a relationship with the Father.

The Father is now able to look upon us and turns to accept us unconditionally. He then turns the heart of the fathers to the children.

"For the Spirit which you have now received is not a spirit of slavery to put you once more in bondage to fear, but you have received the Spirit producing sonship, in (the bliss of) which we cry, Abba! Father!" Romans 8:15. *Amplified New Testament*

FOR YOUR INFORMATION

Incest is found in the Bible in the following scriptures:
> Genesis 19:31-36
> Genesis 35:22
> Genesis 38:16-18
> Genesis 49:4
> II Samuel 13:14, 15
> II Samuel 16:21, 22
> Matthew 14:3,4
> I Corinthians 4:1, 2

It is condemned in the following scriptures:
> Leviticus 18:6-18
> Leviticus 20:11-21
> Deuteronomy 22:30
> Mark 9:42
> Luke 17:1, 2

14

WHERE CAN YOU TURN FOR HELP?

Child Help hotline: (800) 422-4453. It is free to call this number from any phone in the United States. You can call day or night, seven days a week. In other countries, call your local police department, or social service agency. Keep speaking out until you get the help you need.

Eileen McCloy, M.A. (312) 541-7216. She is a Christian therapist specializing in abuse counseling. Write to her at 62 S. Wolf Road, No. 305, Wheeling, IL 60090.

The Chapel of the Air. Information on sexual abuse is offered on tapes, lecture notes, and one-day seminars. Call or write for information. Various resource people have been interviewed on The Chapel of the Air. Write to *National Christian Association, P.O. Box 40945, WA, DC 20016.*

Child Assault Prevention and *Women Against Rape.* Directed by Brad Curl, these activist organizations are committed to defending potential victims of the sex industry. Organizes pickets of people/industries promoting pornography. For example, organizes a yearly picket of *Playboy* magazine's national headquarters in Chicago. Avaiable: "Decency Action Pack Order Form," which offers strategy on how to fight the sex industry. Send $2 for each order form. Write to: Child Assault

Prevention and Women Against Rape, P.O. Box 02084, Columbus, OH 43202. Or call: (614) 291-9751

Parents United. This is a self-help support group associated with counseling centers across U.S. Write to P.O. Box 84353, Los Angeles, CA 90073. Enclose a self-addressed envelope if you wish a response. Or call their hotline at (213) 325-8368

There are also a number of good books that I recommend:

ADULT BOOKS ON SEXUAL ABUSE OF CHILDREN

Adams, Caren and Fay, Jennifer. *No More Secrets: Protecting Your Child From Sexual Assault,* San Luis Obispo, CA: Impact Publishers, 1981.

Armstrong, Louis, *Kiss Daddy Goodnight,* New York: Simon and Schuster, 1978.

Burgess, Ann W. Groth, Nicholas: Holmstrom, Lynda L. and Sgroi, Suzanne, *Sexual Assault of Children and Adolescents,* Lexington, MS: Lexington Books, 1982.

Butler, Sandra, *Conspiracy of Silence: The Trauma of Incest,* San Francisco Volcano Press, Inc., 1978.

Cross, Laurella, *Jenny's New Game,* P.O. Box 4025, Englewood, CO, 80155, 1982.

Fay, Jennifer, *He Told Me Not To Tell,* Renton, WA, King County Rape Relief, 1979.

Herman, Judith Lewis, *Father-Daughter Incest,* Cambridge, MS: Harvard University Press, 1982.

Kerns-Kraizer, Sherryll, *Children Need To Know,* Health Education Systems, 171 Bear Drive, Evergreen, CO 80439, 1983.

Rush, Florence, *The Best Kept Secret: Sexual Abuse of Children,* New York, McGraw-Hill, 1980.

Sanford, Linda, *The Silent Children,* New York: McGraw-Hill, 1982.

Sanford, Lynn. *Come Tell Me Right Away,* Fayetteville, NY: Ed. U. Press, 1983.

Woolfolk, Wm. and Cross, Donna, *Daddy's Little Girl,* Englewood Cliffs, NJ: Prentice-Hall, 1982.

BOOKS FOR CHILDREN AND ADOLESCENTS:

Dayee, Frances S. *Private Zone,* Edmonds, WA: Chas. Franklin Press, 1983.

He Told Me Not To Tell, excellent booklet on the sexual abuse of children with information for anyone concerned. Especially good for helping parents talk to their children. $2.50 order from: King County Rape Relief, 305 S. 43rd, Renton, WA 98055.

Kyte, Kathy S. *Play It Safe: The Kids' Guide To Personal Safety and Crime Prevention*, New York: Alfred A. Kropf, Inc., 1983.

My Very Own Book About Me, Jo Stowell and Mary Dietzel. Illustrated by Sally Pierone, Lutheran Social Services, 1226 Howard, Spokane, WA 99201. Includes a parent's guide. Helps children distinguish between good and bad touching. Instructs them in what to do if someone approaches them in this way.

National Committee for Prevention of Child Abuse, *Sexual Abuse Prevention Material*, Box 2866, Chicago, IL 60690. This packet costs $2 and is a listing of books, films and programs on the subject.

Spider-Man and Power Pack, P.O. Box 94283, Chicago, IL 60690. The comic book, which has been reviewed by several child sexual abuse experts and endorsed by the National Education Association, is being published by the Marvel Comics Group in cooperation with the National Committee for Prevention of Child Abuse. To order, send $1 tax-free donation check or money order and your name and address.

Top Secret, King County Rape Relief, 305 South 43rd, Renton, WA 98055. (Workbook for adolescents).

Wachter, Oralee, *No More Secrets For Me*, Boston, Little, Brown and Company, 1983.

We Can Combat Child Sexual Abuse and *Child Pornography* by Shirley O'Brien. Extensive research done on these issues. Write to her to learn how to receive these books by writing to: Coopertive Extension Service, University of Arizona, College of Agriculture, Tucson, AZ 85721

What if ... I say NO, work booklet designed to teach young children about sexual abuse and how to protect themselves. $3.50 plus $3 shipping. Order from M. H. Cap and Co., P.O. Box 3584, Bakersfield, CA 03385-3584.

AFTERWORD

It was a hot summer afternoon and I had taken off from work early to meet with my lawyer and to sign the final draft of the divorce papers.

I signed the papers and as I stood to leave, I wiped the tears from my eyes.

My lawyer walked over to me and said, "Are you sure this is what you want?"

"Yes," I replied. "I never thought it would come to this or that so many things could go wrong in one person's life — but yes, this is what I want."

Then I added, "And I promise you that five years from now I will be proud of what I am doing."

I really was surprised at what I had said — but she came over and hugged me — and I left.

How would I ever be proud of what I had done — divorcing my husband — because he abused my children? The furthest thing from my mind was being able to look back on this day and at this mess and say, "Praise God, I did live through these difficult and impossible situations and I am proud of what has been accomplished."

It really didn't take five years to begin to see progress in each of us — especially me. But at this writing it has been five years since I stood in the lawyer's office and I can see that I had no real concept of what I was saying at the time — no concept of what would be required to survive. But whether it was a self-fulfilling prophecy or whether God was creating the fruit of my lips as in Isaiah 57:19 — I don't know. But I can honestly say that God has gone past my fondest dreams or my greatest desires in what he has accomplished in my life as well as the lives of my children, giving me reason to be proud of what I did that summer afternoon in the lawyer's office.

Everyday I find more evidence of the greatness of God in my life and I know that if He were not willing to change me and if I were not willing and ready for a complete remodeling and renewal — nothing would have been accomplished with my divorce.

If you will cooperate with God, there are things he can and will change and bring to pass in your life which are even past believing for today — but God knows that beauty of being perfected in his image and will show you enough of a glimpse to increase your faith in Him to bring it to pass.

I used to think that if I could only have a reasonable working relationship with my children, God would have answered my prayers. But just to demonstrate how much more he planned to provide me with — a few months ago Debbie wrote me this note along with some baby pictures of my grandson.

> *Dear Mom,*
>
> *Thanks a lot for helping us out — if I didn't have a good friend and mother like you to call on, I wouldn't have the guts or will power to stick it out. I really appreciate you and I love you so much. As time goes by you grow more precious to me and I love you more and more. I guess that's all I have to tell you because I can't write all I want to tell you. I love you and miss you.*
>
> > *Your loving daughter,*
> > *Debbie*

That is what five years of perseverance, hard work and a total reliance on God can do.

ORDER FORM

Please find enclosed my prepaid order:

BOOKS *from Meridel and Jay Rawlings*
(for postage and handling add $1 per book):

_____ **Fishers and Hunters.** Visits to Jewish communities around the world encouraging them to return to Zion. Large format edition, $6.95 Abridged edition, $3.95.

_____ **Gates of Brass.** On the plight of Soviet Jews including secret material smuggled out of Russia. "Behind the scenes" story of film by the same title, $5.95.

FILMS & VIDEOS *from Meridel and Jay Rawlings*
(for postage and handling, add $2):

Apples of Gold. Modern History of Israel (78 minutes)
_____ Film, $95 _____ VHS video, $85 ____ BETA video, $85
Gates of Brass Plight of Soviet Jews, (54 minutes)
_____ VHS video, $75   _____BETA video, $75
Lebanon & the Middle East: the Untold Story (28 minutes)
_____ VHS video, $55   _____BETA video, $55

AMOUNT ENCLOSED: _____

Name _____

Address _____

City _____ State ____ Zip _____

ORDER FROM:

In Israel—

Meridel & Jay Rawlings
Box 8232,
Jerusalem 91081
Telephone (02) 246027
Telex 26144 BXJMIL ext. 7276

In the United States —

Meridel &Jay Rawlings
Box 24630
Dallas, Texas 75224
Telephone (214) 948-3411

In Canada—

Meridel & Jay Rawlings
243 Broadway
Orangeville, Ontario L9W 1K6
Telephone (519) 941-4310

MORE FAITH-BUILDING BOOKS
FROM HUNTINGTON HOUSE

America Betrayed! by Marlin Maddoux. This hard-hitting book exposes forces in our country which seek to destroy the family, the schools and our values. This book details how the news media manipulates your mind. Marlin Maddoux is the host of the popular, national radio talk show "Point of View."

A Reasonable Reason to Wait, by Jacob Aranza, is a frank, definitive discussion on premarital sex — from the biblical viewpoint. God speaks specifically about premarital sex, according to the author. The Bible also provides a healing message for those already sexually involved before marriage. This book is a must reading for every young person — and also for parents — who really want to know the biblical truth on this important subject.

Backward Masking Unmasked, by Jacob Aranza. Rock'n'roll music affects tens of millions of young people and adults in America and around the world. This music is laced with lyrics exalting drugs, the occult, immorality, homosexuality, violence and rebellion. But there is a more sinister danger in this music, according to the author. It's called "backward masking." Numerous rock groups employ this mind-influencing technique in their recordings. Teenagers by the millions — who spend hours each day listening to rock music — aren't even aware the messages are there. The author clearly exposes these dangers.

Backward Masking Unmasked, (cassette tape) by Jacob Aranza. Hear actual satanic messages and judge for yourself.

Beast, by Dan Betzer. This is the fictional story of the rise to power of a future world dictator — the Antichrist. This novel plots a dark web of intrigue beginning with the suicide-death of Adolf Hitler who believed he had been chosen to be the world dictator. Yet, in his last days, he spoke of "the man who will come after me." Several decades later that man, Jacque Catroux, head of the European economic system, appears on the world scene. He had been born the day Hitler died, conceived by the seed of Lucifer himself. In articulate prose, the author describes the "disappearance" of Christians from the earth; horror and hopelessness following that event; and the bitter agony of life on earth after all moral and spiritual restraints are removed.

Computers and the Beast of Revelation, by Dr. David Webber and Noah Hutchings. The authors masterfully explain the arrival of this great age of information, particularly relating to computers, in light of Bible prophecy. They share information about computer control, computer networks, computer spies and the ultimate computer. Today there are signs all around us that computers are merging all economic transactions into a single. all-knowledgeable system and all nations into one economic system. For centuries Bible scholars have wondered how Revelation 13 could ever be fulfilled: When would some kind of image or machine command everyone in the world to work or buy and sell with code marks and numbers? This book answers that question.

Devil Take the Youngest by Winkie Pratney. This book reveals the war on children being waged in America and the world today. Pratney, a world-renowned author, teacher and conference speaker, says a spirit of Moloch is loose in the land. The author relates parallels of ancient Moloch worship — where children were sacrificed screaming into his burning fire — to today's tragic killing and kidnapping of children. This timely book says the war on children has its roots in the occult.

Globalism: America's Demise, by William Bowen, Jr. The Globalists — some of the most powerful people on earth — have plans to totally eliminate God, the family, and the United States as we know it today. Globalism is the vehicle the humanists are using to implement their secular humanistic philosophy to bring about their one-world government. The four goals of Globalism are: 1) a one-world government; 2) a new world religion; 3) a new economic system; 4) a new race of people for the new world order. This book alerts Christians to what Globalists have planned for them.

Hearts on Fire, by Jimmy Phillips. What is God doing throughout the world? Where is revival taking place? What is the heart's cry of the people? Phillips answers these and other important questions in this delightful book. As you read his story, your heart will be set on fire.

Honor Thy Father? by Meridel Rawlings. Incest destroys the seemingly normal family of a small-town pastor who has hidden his darkest secret even from his wife. But there is hope and recovery through the love of Jesus.

How to Cope When You Can't by Don Gossett is a guide to dealing with the everyday stresses and pressures of life. Gossett, a well-known Christian author and evangelist, draws from many personal experiences in this book which brings hope and encouragement for victory in our Lord. The author deals with such contemporary subjects as coping with guilt, raising children, financial difficulties, poverty, a sectarian spirit, the devil's devices, pride, fear and inadequacy, sickness, sorrow, enemies and other real problems.

More Rock, Country & Backward Masking Unmasked by Jacob Aranza. Aranza's first book, *Backward Masking Unmasked,* was a national bestseller. It clearly exposed the backward satanic messages included in a lot of rock and roll music. Now, in the sequel, Aranza gives a great deal of new information on backward messages. Also, for the first time in Christian literature, he takes a hard look at the content, meaning and dangers of country music. "Rock, though filled with satanism, sex and drugs ... has a hard time keeping up with the cheatin', drinkin' and one-night stands that continue to dominate country music," the author says.

Murdered Heiress ... Living Witness, by Dr. Petti Wagner. The victim of a sinister kidnapping and murder plot, the Lord miraculously gave her life back to her. Dr. Wagner — heiress to a large fortune — was kidnapped, tortured, beaten, electrocuted and died. A doctor signed her death certificate, yet she lives today!

Rest From the Quest, by Elissa Lindsey McClain. This is the candid account of a former New Ager who spent the first 29 years of her life in the New Age Movement, the occult and Eastern mysticism. This is an incredible inside look at what really goes on in the New Age Movement.

The Great Falling Away Today. by Milton Green. This renowned speaker shows the joy and peace that comes through deliverance — and cites what the Bible says about the future of an unrepentant church.

The Hidden Dangers of the Rainbow, by Constance Cumbey. A national #1 bestseller, this is a vivid exposé of the New Age Movement which is dedicated to wiping out Christianity and establishing a one-world order. This movement — a vast network of tens of thousands of occultic and other organizations — meets the test of prophecy concerning the Antichrist.

The Miracle of Touching, by Dr. John Hornbrook. Most everyone enjoys the special attention that a loving touch brings. Throughout this encouraging book the author explains what touching others through love — under the careful guidance of the Lord Jesus Christ — can accomplish. Dr. Hornbrook urges Christians to reach out and touch someone — family members, friends, prisoners — and do it to the glory of God, physically, emotionally and spiritually.

The Twisted Cross, by Joseph Carr. One of the most important works of our decade, The Twisted Cross documents occult and demonic influences on Adolf Hitler which led to the killing of more than 6 million Jews.

Where Were You When I Was Hurting? by Nicky Cruz. Former New York City teen gang leader Nicky Cruz takes the reader on a gripping, emotion-packed trek into earthquake-shattered Mexico City, into drug-plagued Budapest, Hungary, into Satanist-infested Asuncion, Paraguay, South America, and back into the streets of New York and Chicago with the message of God's healing that comes when we are willing to give up our bitterness and simply forgive. A powerful teaching and witnessing tool from one of America's all-time bestselling authors.

Who Will Rise Up? by Jed Smock. This is the incredible — and sometimes hilarious — story of Jed Smock, who with his wife, Cindy, has preached the uncompromising gospel on the malls and lawns of hundreds of university campuses throughout this land. They have been mocked, rocked, stoned, mobbed, beaten, jailed, cursed and ridiculed by the students. Yet this former university professor and his wife have seen the miracle-working power of God transform thousands of lives on university campuses.

Yes, send me the following books:

___ copy (copies) of	America Betrayed! @ $5.95		$ ___ =
___ copy (copies) of	A Reasonable Reason To Wait @ $4.95		$ ___ =
___ copy (copies) of	Backward Masking Unmasked @ $5.95		$ ___ =
___ copy (copies) of	Backward Masking Unmasked Cassette Tape @ $6.95		$ ___ =
___ copy (copies) of	Computers and the Beast of Revelation @ $6.95		$ ___ =
___ copy (copies) of	Devil Take the Youngest @ $6.95		$ ___ =
___ copy (copies) of	Edmund Burke and the Natural Law @ $7.95		$ ___ =
___ copy (copies) of	Globalism: America's Demise @ $6.95		$ ___ =
___ copy (copies) of	God's Timetable for the 1980's @ $5.95		$ ___ =
___ copy (copies) of	Hearts on Fire @ $5.95		$ ___ =
___ copy (copies) of	Honor Thy Father @ $6.95		$ ___ =
___ copy (copies) of	How to Cope When You Can't @ $6.95		$ ___ =
___ copy (copies) of	More Rock, Country & Backward Masking Unmasked @ $5.95		$ ___ =
___ copy (copies) of	More Rock, Country & Backward Masking Unmasked Tape @ $6.95		$ ___ =
___ copy (copies) of	Murdered Heiress ... Living Witness @ $6.95		$ ___ =
___ copy (copies) of	Natalie @ $4.95		$ ___ =
___ copy (copies) of	Need a Miracle? @ $5.95		$ ___ =
___ copy (copies) of	Rest From the Quest @ $5.95		$ ___ =
___ copy (copies) of	The Agony of Deception @ $6.95		$ ___ =
___ copy (copies) of	The Divine Connection @ $4.95		$ ___ =
___ copy (copies) of	The Hidden Dangers of the Rainbow @ $6.95		$ ___ =
___ copy (copies) of	The Great Falling Away Today @ $6.95		$ ___ =
___ copy (copies) of	The Hidden Dangers of the Rainbow Seminar Tapes @ $19.95		$ ___ =
___ copy (copies) of	The Miracle of Touching @ $5.95		$ ___ =
___ copy (copies) of	The Twisted Cross @ $7.95		$ ___ =
___ copy (copies) of	Where Were You When I Was Hurting? @ $6.95		$ ___ =
___ copy (copies) of	Who Will Rise Up? @ $5.95		$ ___ =

AT BOOKSTORES EVERYWHERE or order direct from Huntington House, P.O. Box 53788, Lafayette, LA 70505

Send check/money order or for faster service VISA/Mastercard orders call toll-free 1-800-572-8213. Add: Freight and handling, $1.00 for the first book ordered, 50¢ for each additional book.

Enclosed is $ ___ including postage.

Name ___

Address ___

City ___ State and ZIP ___